How to start motor racing

2001 Edition

Produced for the
Association
of
Racing Drivers
Schools

Supported by
Demon Tweeks

t*f*m
Publishing Limited

Published by TFM Publishing Ltd
Brimstree View
Kemberton
Shifnal
Shropshire
TF11 9LL

Tel: 01952 586408
Fax: 01952 587654
e-mail: nikki@tfmpub.freeserve.co.uk
Web site: www.tfmpublishing.co.uk

Design and layout: Nikki Bramhill

First edition January 1998
Second edition December 1998
Third edition December 1999
Fourth edition December 2000

ISBN 1 903378 03 6

Foreword
By Paul O'Brien -
Chairman of ARDS

Many drivers dream of taking the wheel of a racing car but have difficulty making their dream a reality. Perhaps deterred by lack of funds, other demands on their time, or simply not knowing how to go about it, their enjoyment of motorsport never goes beyond enthusiastic spectating or avidly reading the motorsport press.

But this fully updated 2001 edition of 'How to start motor racing' from ARDS - the Association of Racing Drivers' Schools - shows you not only that it can be done, but takes you, step-by-step, through how it can be done.

You don't have to sacrifice your whole life and family future to your motor racing ambitions (unless your goal is to make it all the way to the top). Why not simply enjoy the excitement of learning to drive a racing car on track? You can choose how fast and how far you want to progress with the guidance, support and encouragement of one of the ARDS schools.

Several schools run their own racing teams or can put you on track with other reputable teams if you are aiming for a different formula. Remember that all ARDS instructors are themselves racing drivers and are always ready to talk to you about your plans.

Please don't put off your enjoyment of race driving another day. Enjoy reading this book - and good luck with your motor racing!

Paul O'Brien

The editorial team

Nigel Greensall - a very successful racer and instructor who, during 1997 and 1998, was the fastest British national racing driver. Racing a Formula One Tyrrell in the BOSS series, Greensall smashed five outright circuit records. He has numerous race wins and several championship titles to his credit and successfully finished the 1997 Daytona 24 Hour race.

Don Lawrence - a marshal and senior official with more than 30 year's experience of race organisation. Former Chief Observer for the British Racing Drivers' Club and former National Training Officer of the British Motor Racing Marshals Club.

Paul Lawrence - freelance journalist and author specialising in national motor racing. Regular contributor to Autosport and Motoring News, with more than 20 years experience in the sport.

The overview -
you really can do it!

Motor racing is a wonderful sport. In our opinion, it is the best sport in the world! Every weekend of the season, hundreds of racers compete in a vast array of cars at race meetings up and down Britain. Driving a racing car is one of the most exhilarating experiences in the world and racing against a host of rivals is among the most memorable of all leisure activities. Fun, excitement, elation, camaraderie, escape from the everyday pressures of life and the desire for success are just some of the reasons why people go motor racing.

The thrill of racing against other cars whilst coping with the demands of the race track has few rivals and can be very addictive. The sheer thrill of driving on the limit and pushing yourself to find new limits all the time, whilst getting the most out of the car cannot be over-stated.

For the successful, the elation of victory is unforgettable. For others, the sheer pleasure of competing is sufficient. But for everyone, the excitement of pushing to the limits of either man or machine (or both!) is one of the key motivations for going racing.

Much is talked about the prohibitive cost of the sport and there can be no doubt that, at the higher levels, the sport is very expensive. However, in Chapters 3 and 7, we hope to demonstrate that motor racing is well within the reach of those on normal incomes and not just the very wealthy or the lucky few who have landed a big sponsor. Complete cars ready to race in some of the low-cost classes can be bought for less than £3000.

Aspiring racing drivers fall broadly into two categories. There are the determined and ambitious who are hoping to make a career as a professional racing driver with, perhaps, Grand Prix racing as their ultimate goal. However, the greater number are those seeking to make motor racing their prime leisure activity. For them, the choice is wide and there is a type of racing to suit just about every taste and pocket.

Whichever category you fall into, we are sure that this book has something for you.

In producing the 2001 edition of this book, ARDS hopes to save newcomers from some of the pitfalls and problems that typically beset novices as they take their first steps in the sport. We cannot cover every situation that you may encounter, but by publishing this guide, we aim to take much of the mystery out of a sport that can seem like an impenetrable maze to those on the outside.

Every weekend in Britain, drivers are competing - and winning - at modest cost in a wide range of cars. If you thought racing was beyond your budget, be prepared to think again, you really can do it!

What this book is about

In buying this book, you have taken the first step on the road towards starting racing. We hope that when you have digested the information in the following pages, you will decide to go ahead and start racing. It is not a difficult process to follow, but there obviously have to be rules and controls to govern the sport. Motor racing in Britain has an excellent safety record, protected by the on-going work of the MSA (the sport's governing body).

Later in this book, we will cover the information you need to know about getting to the stage of competing in your first race. We have constructed the book to flow in a logical sequence, from your first experience at a racing school through to taking part in a race. There is a lot of information to cover, and you may not need to digest it all in one go. So, we have organised the book in such a way that you can dip into the parts that you need at any time. We have built in 'sign-posts' to lead you to related sections and at the start of each chapter is a synopsis of the information it contains.

Chapter 1 covers a basic introduction to the sport and how it is organised. More knowledgeable readers may already be familiar with this information. Chapter 1 then goes on to explain the role of ARDS (the Association of Racing Drivers' Schools) and the work of the racing school.

If you have already decided that you want to start racing, but don't know about the process for getting started, **Chapter 2** explains the route to gaining the necessary racing licence and getting equipped to start.

For people now ready to start making decisions about where to race and in what type of car, **Chapter 3** covers essential information about racing classes, buying and preparing a race car and making sure that the driver is ready for the challenge that lays ahead! This section links to **Chapter 7**, which is a unique reference index of all British racing classes and a detailed listing of every championship. Careful study of these chapters should help you make the right decision about where to start racing.

Once you are ready to enter your first race, **Chapter 4** tells you all about the first race meeting. There is a lot of information to absorb about the 'big day' and we have broken the chapter down into easily digestible sections.

There are a number of excellent books in existence about the technicalities of race car engineering. However, in **Chapter 5** we have endeavoured to provide an introduction to some of the essentials including tyres, suspension and aerodynamics. If you find that you want to know more, one of the specialist motoring bookshops will be able to offer a range of titles that cover these topics in great detail.

Sooner or later, you may consider the need to attract sponsorship for your racing programme. **Chapter 6** offers an introduction to sponsor-hunting and some common-sense advice about how to start this often arduous task. Once again, dedicated books on the subject will be essential reading for those determined to attract substantial levels of support.

Chapter 7, as previously mentioned, is the complete breakdown of all UK classes of racing and championships, while **Chapter 8** details items like useful addresses, publications and web sites, as well as the directory of ARDS-recognised racing schools.

Please now read on. There is much to absorb, and we hope that this book will be a source of information and advice throughout your introduction to the sport that so many of us love.

PAUL LAWRENCE
EDITOR

Contents

CHAPTER 4 - THE FIRST RACE MEETING

CHAPTER 5 - GETTING THE BEST FROM YOUR CAR

CHAPTER 6 - SO YOU NEED A SPONSOR!

CHAPTER 7 - BRITISH RACING CATEGORIES AND
CHAPMIONSHIP

CHAPTER 8 - APPENDICES

Index of advertisers

CHAPTER 1
THE FIRST STEPS

IN THIS CHAPTER

1.1 THE BIG PICTURE

➢ A run down on the structure of motorsport both world-wide and in the UK.

➢ The role of the MSA.

➢ The major international classes.

➢ The depth of the sport in Britain.

1.2 THE ASSOCIATION OF RACING DRIVERS' SCHOOLS

➢ The role of ARDS

➢ Member schools

➢ Instructor licensing

1.3 BACK TO SCHOOL

➢ What the schools offer

➢ The first lesson

➢ Racing with a school

1.4 CHOOSING A SCHOOL

➢ The ARDS standard

1.1 THE BIG PICTURE

Beware. Motor sport can be addictive. It has often been said that the sport should carry a government health warning. Once hooked, participants, be they racers, team members, officials or fans, can find it very difficult to escape the clutches of a sport that can take you from the heights of exhilaration to the depths of despair. Sometimes in the space of a few minutes. But, it is a great sport that provides excitement for thousands. If you are ultimately fortunate enough to compete, you will remember your racing for the rest of your life.

Globally, all motorsport is governed by the FIA (Federation Internationale de l'Automobile) from its office in Geneva. The responsibility for governing the sport nationally is devolved to individual bodies in each country. For Great Britain, it is the Royal Automobile Club which, in turn, entrusts this duty to a separate body, the Motor Sports Association.

The MSA (as it is known) is responsible for all aspects of regulation of motor sport. Its duties and powers are extensive and cover things like licensing of competitors, inspection and licensing of venues, control of technical regulations for vehicles and monitoring the organisation and running of events. With wide-ranging powers, the MSA is a professional body committed to the cause of ever-safer competition and the protection of the sport. Its revenue is largely generated from the licence fees paid by competitors.

While the MSA is concerned with the overall control of the sport, the promotion of motor racing in Britain rests with the circuit owners and major organising clubs. There are a number of relationships between the circuit owners and organising clubs but, ultimately, all are working towards increased crowd attendance and more participants. This is a subject we will expand on in later chapters.

To set the scene, let's start at the top, for that is what most people perceive the sport to be about. At the pinnacle of world motor sport is Formula 1 Grand Prix racing, where the very best drivers in the sport compete for the biggest prize of all. Top teams like Williams, Ferrari and McLaren spend many millions of pounds each year and employ hundreds of people in their quest for success. The fastest drivers of the current era can earn more than a million pounds for each race on the Grand Prix calendar. The races are seen by billions of viewers around the world and the top names are world superstars.

However, while Grand Prix racing is hugely popular throughout much of the world, it has never enjoyed major popularity in North America. Instead, single-seater racing across the Atlantic is dominated by the Champ cars. Though less technically sophisticated than Formula 1 cars, these cars are just as fast, and lap the banked oval tracks in America at average speeds of well over 200mph.

Away from single-seater racing, two forms of motor racing have major global importance. Through the 1990s, Touring Car racing boomed in many countries as motor manufacturers took the opportunity to prove and promote their products in fierce competition. Led by the highly successful British Touring Car Championship, the 'Super Touring' category - as the class is known - was adopted by many countries, notably throughout Europe and in the Asia-Pacific region.

However, at the turn of the decade, Super Touring was starting to wane as cost spiralled and manufacturers pulled out. For 2001, the British Touring Car Championship will switch to a new development of the Super Touring regulations, with cars returning to a specification closer to the Super Production category. Development of suspension and brakes is permitted, but the cars remain visually similar to the models in the showroom.

For 2001, the Super Production cars previously racing in the National Saloon Championship will form a permanent class within the BTCC, thus ensuring good grids of closely-matched saloons.

Running alongside rounds of the British Touring Car Championship is a package of support races, many of which enjoy manufacturer support. This package of national championships appears at each Touring Car meeting and will be covered more fully in Chapter 7.

See Chapter 7

Each Touring Car meeting features two rounds of the BTCC, the Sprint Race and the Feature race. These races are separated by a couple of hours to give teams the opportunity to repair cars that suffer mechanical problems or accident damage in the Sprint Race.

Sports car racing - topped by the world famous Le Mans 24 hour race - has two distinct elements. GT racing is for race developed cars based on road-going GT cars such as the Porsche and Chrysler Viper. Sports prototype racing, meanwhile, is for purpose-built open two-seat type cars and there are international championships for both types of car.

These four categories, Formula 1, Champ Cars, Touring Cars and Sports Cars, are the most important in world motor racing. Beneath them are literally dozens of classes, some purely national, some pan-European and a few world-wide. Among those that have championships in a number of countries are junior single-seater classes like Formula Ford and Formula 3 which are recognised steps on the motor racing ladder for aspiring stars.

Many youngsters start racing in karts where they can begin their competitive career at just eight years old. Indeed, most successful single-seater racers will have started in karting and many of the drivers on a current day Grand Prix grid will have a strong karting pedigree. Our sister publication, 'How to start kart racing' covers this in detail.

At 16, they can progress into cars (providing they have proved themselves in karting) and then graduate up through the single-seater classes. There is no mandatory route through the junior single-seater classes, but Formula 3 is widely considered to be an important rung on the ladder, where young hopefuls race high-tech two-litre single-seaters. A few drivers like Jenson Button jump straight from F3 into Grand Prix racing.

The next step is Formula 3000 where they race three-litre racing cars in International competition. For the very best young talents, Formula 3000 is the final step before Grand Prix racing, but it is a tough journey and only a very few ever make it all the way to the top.

Britain enjoys a prominent position in world motor racing. Most of the Grand Prix teams are based in England, with the notable exception of

Ferrari, and many of the world's single-seater racing cars are built in Britain. The sheer depth of engineering expertise in this country means that motor sport earns considerable export income. More than 50,000 people are employed in the UK directly through motor sport. It is big business and Britain is the world centre for the sport.

THE SINGLE-SEATER LADDER

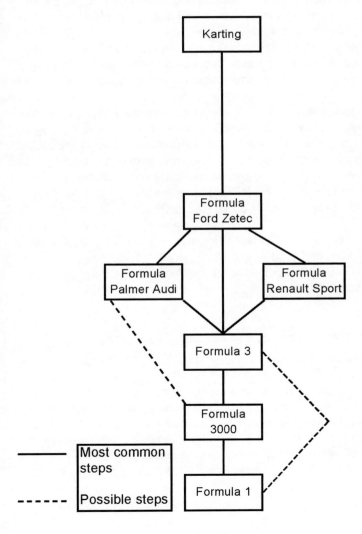

Race car manufacturers like Lola, Reynard and Van Diemen are all British companies and export their products all over the world. Equally, ambitious young racing drivers regularly come to Britain to try and prove themselves in their formative years. Just one such driver was Ayrton Senna, who came from Brazil as a young racer and made his name racing in the junior single-seater classes in Britain.

Reflecting the position of British motor racing is the quantity and quality of racing to be found on every weekend of the season. Between the beginning of March and mid-November, there are over 230 race meetings in Britain at 16 permanent race tracks. The scale of these meetings is vast; from the showcase British Grand Prix meeting to a club meeting arranged primarily for the members of the organising club.

A handful of race meetings will be international events featuring rounds of international championships, while approximately 26 will be major promoted events run under the umbrella of British Motorsport Promoters (BMP). This group, which emerged in 2000, is formed by the leading UK circuits and has now developed two major British racing packages. The BTCC is one and the emergent PowerTour is the other, with PowerTour headlined by the British Formula 3 and British GT Championships.

A number of meetings will be for drivers racing classic, historic and vintage machinery and others will cater for the 140 championships currently found in British national racing. For most people, however, their first on-track experience will come through a racing school.

1.2 THE ASSOCIATION OF RACING DRIVERS' SCHOOLS

Twenty years ago, there were only three or four racing schools in Britain. Virtually all of their business came from ambitious individuals who dreamt of going racing. However, through the 1980s, the number and range of schools expanded to meet ever-growing demand, particularly from businesses that realised that a day driving on a race track was an excellent way of entertaining clients. Now, virtually every circuit in Britain is host to a racing school.

The MSA recognised that this expansion could lead to varying standards across the industry and worked in conjunction with the most respected schools to create an industry body that would set and maintain appropriate standards of tuition and operational safety.

See Chapter 8.1

One of the major functions of the association has been, in conjunction with the MSA, to create a licensing system for racing school instructors. Currently, nearly 400 instructors have an ARDS licence. All of them are required to have relevant racing experience and many of them are professional or semi-professional racing drivers.

By creating the instructor licensing system, ARDS has been able to steadily improve the standard of on-track tuition by a programme of training and development for the instructors. Not only does this benefit the customer who is assured a high-standard of professionalism, but also the individual instructor who has a qualification that is recognised throughout the industry. Many motor manufacturers and corporate clients now specify a requirement for ARDS-licensed instructors at all time, for tuition both on and off the race track.

In 1992, the MSA and ARDS took another important step with the creation of the Novice Driver Training Course. For some time, there had been concern that novice drivers could start racing without any test of their ability or understanding of the basic rules of the sport. The now-mandatory Novice Driver Training Course (NDTC) was developed as a result and is covered in more detail in Chapter 2.1.

See Chapter 2.1

1.3   BACK TO SCHOOL

BACK TO SCHOOL

The ARDS-recognised schools fulfil many different roles. For the great majority of the 120,000 customers who visit a school each year, it is a unique day out that allows them to experience the thrill of driving on a race track. Frequently, that will be the extent of their active involvement in motorsport and all ARDS schools are geared up to provide half-day or full-day 'driving experience' type activities.

But the schools do not only provide on-track driving. Increasingly, there is a demand, particularly from large companies, for driving instruction that is more relevant to every day road driving. Often these sessions are arranged for company car drivers and can include skid-car sessions and defensive driving training.

The third element of racing school business is where the whole industry was founded; people who want to learn to be racing drivers. Most ARDS schools offer training that is geared towards taking complete novices to the stage where they are ready to start their racing career. The length and content (and therefore cost!) of these courses will vary from school to school and, in several instances, can be completed by the opportunity to take part in a race organised solely by the school for its pupils.

For pupils who show particular promise, several ARDS schools now operate scholarship schemes which can make it possible for star pupils to compete in their first race or races with financial and technical support from the school.

See Chapter 2.5

School courses can be tailored to suit pupils with ambitions in either single-seater or saloon car racing. Once the initial courses have been completed, ARDS schools can then provide one-to-one tuition and coaching with senior instructors for those who wish to hone their newly-acquired skills.

This intensive tuition is not, however, limited to drivers in the very early stages of their careers. Often, experienced racing drivers from classes such as Formula 3, will call upon the services of the schools to help them master a particular circuit in preparation for a forthcoming race. As in all walks of life, the person who thinks they know it all can often be proved spectacularly wrong!

Whatever your particular agenda, an ARDS-recognised school is the place to start – and perhaps complete – your active involvement in motor racing. For those with ambition to actually race, schools can offer customers the opportunity to progress from being a complete novice to the point of being a competent racer taking part in a race.

So what should you expect when you arrive at a racing school? Typically, the training will start with a classroom briefing where a senior instructor will take you through the programme for the day and brief you on the essential safety aspects of the session. Suitable helmets will be provided, while soft shoes are strongly recommended.

The briefing will present you with a considerable amount of information in a fairly short space of time but it will all be relevant and important. It will include information about flag signals, how to join and leave the circuit and rules about overtaking. If you are unsure about any aspect of the briefing, you should ask questions. The senior instructor will always be pleased to answer questions, either during the briefing or privately afterwards.

At most, but not all schools, you will gain your first experience of the circuit in a race-prepared saloon car. Your instructor – who will be an experienced racing driver – will show you the correct line, braking points, gear changing points and general circuit technique. In a couple of cases, however, you get straight into a single-seater.

The lesson will show you how to take the corners correctly and how to balance the car under braking and through the corner. 'Slow in, fast out' is an expression you will probably hear in relation to cornering technique.

Depending upon the type of course, you may then progress into a single-seater racing car. The instructor will give a full briefing relevant to the particular type of car. Modern racing cars have fairly cramped cockpits but the school will cater for all sizes and shapes of pupil (within reason!) and you will be matched to a car that is set up to accommodate you. However, should you be more than 6ft6" tall or weigh more than 16 stones, it is worth checking with the school beforehand that they can accommodate you.

Don't forget that in many single-seater racing cars, the gear lever is on the right. At first you may find the clutch pedal very heavy, but after a few laps you should become accustomed to the very different feel of a racing clutch.

Once onto the circuit, with the engine right behind you and the wind rushing at you, it is a unique feeling. Being able to see the wheels is a novel experience along with the small steering wheel which needs only a slight movement to apply lock. However, by remembering the words of the instructor, you will get into a rhythm and each lap will come more and more naturally. Circuit driving demands intense concentration to get it right so don't be surprised if you make a mistake or two. This is quite normal, and the school will have allowed for this when planning the session.

1.4 CHOOSING A SCHOOL

The choice of where to go for tuition will be influenced by several factors, the most important one being location. The best advice is to check the list of ARDS-recognised schools in Chapter 7.1 and select the one that is most accessible for you. They all operate to the same high standards and, though each school has its own individuality, ARDS membership is a guarantee of high standards of safety, tuition and customer-care.

Importantly, the ARDS schools all operate at circuits that have MSA circuit licences. In short, this means that the circuit you will be driving on is annually inspected by MSA officials and has met their criteria for holding race meetings. You would be very unfortunate to have an accident during a school lesson, but if you did, the circuit safety facilities will meet the high standards required for race meetings.

Further, the racing cars used by ARDS-recognised schools are periodically inspected by a senior MSA scrutineer who will have checked the car's suitability for circuit use. This is similar to an MOT for a road car, but concentrates on the elements of the car that are particularly important for on-track safety.

CHAPTER 2
SO YOU WANT TO GO RACING!

IN THIS CHAPTER

2.1 THE NOVICE DRIVER TRAINING COURSE
- ➤ The 'Go Racing' pack
- ➤ The content of the Novice Driver Training Course
- ➤ The examination

2.2 RACE LICENCES
- ➤ Applying for a licence
- ➤ The types of race licence
- ➤ Upgrading licences
- ➤ Licence fees

2.3 MEDICALS
- ➤ The requirement
- ➤ The test
- ➤ Medical fees

2.4 BUYING RACEWEAR
- ➤ The standards
- ➤ Crash helmets
- ➤ Overalls and other racewear
- ➤ Looking after your racewear

2.5 RACING SCHOLARSHIPS
- ➢ What to look for in a scholarship
- ➢ What to avoid!

2.6 INSURANCE
- ➢ On and off-track insurance for racing cars
- ➢ Personal insurance

2.7 THE OFFICIALS OF THE MEETING
- ➢ The key officials
- ➢ Their responsibility and power
- ➢ Driver penalties
- ➢ The scrutineers
- ➢ Marshals

2.1   The Novice Driver Training Course

Once you have made the decision that you want to take your fledgling racing career a stage further, there are, of course, a number of things that you need to do. In this chapter we will take you from the beginning through to the point where you are ready to enter your very first race. This process can be completed in a matter of days, if necessary. The speed with which you progress through the various steps is entirely down to you and your particular situation.

Before anyone can go motor racing in Britain, they need to obtain a competition licence from the MSA. Although a straight-forward process, this involves several steps. The MSA will supply a 'Go Racing' starter pack which provides plenty of useful information about making a start in the sport. This is also available from Demon Tweeks. In the Go Racing pack is the race licence application form and a list of ARDS-recognised schools. Then, a medical examination is required to ensure that the candidate is fit enough to go racing.

See Chapter 2.2 & 2.3

Next comes a course at one of the racing schools that are recognised by ARDS. The 'Novice Driver Training Course' is a mandatory step for intending racers. During this course, the candidate will be instructed in basic racing skills and complete a written test to check their understanding of essential safety regulations, flag signals and basic car control.

When you attend for the NDTC course you will need to take your full road driving licence and the race licence application form with the medical certificate section already completed. If you are 16 or over and have been competing in a kart for at least 12 months, and have obtained six signatures on your kart competition licence, you can attend an ARDS school to take the NDTC even though you will not have a full road driving licence. But, don't forget that if you are under 18, you must have parental approval. From January 2000, drivers could qualify for a licence from age 14 under special circumstances. This particularly relates to the T-Car initiative organised by the BRSCC.

During the NDTC course, you will take to the track with a senior instructor where your driving will be assessed with the emphasis on correct technique and application of the classroom teaching.

After the on-track session, you have to take a written exam. To pass the test, you must score at least 65% in the driving assessment, 100% in the first section of the written assessment and 50% in the second section of the written assessment. However, passing the test alone is not necessarily enough as approval from the senior instructor is still required. This requirement places a responsibility on the ARDS school and the senior instructor to satisfy themselves that the candidate is fit to race and has sufficient understanding of the rules of the sport. It is in the best interests of the candidate and existing racers that this decision is not taken lightly, as an irresponsible or ill-equipped driver is a potential hazard to fellow racers.

The video that comes as part of the 'Go Racing' pack covers all the points you need to know to pass the NDTC and it is worth watching the video several times before going for the test. The video runs for around 30 minutes and covers a host of information that will be useful during the NDTC and as you make a start in the sport.

There is nothing complex or tricky about the NDTC, but you will need to show a reasonable understanding of the basic rules of the sport to be successful. An important element of the test is to check the candidates knowledge of the flag signals used throughout the sport. If you should fail the assessment, the course can be re-taken and you should discuss this with the school on the day of the test.

If, after watching the video, you feel that you may not be properly prepared to take the test, make contact with the school where you intend to go for the NDTC test. If you express your concerns to the school, they should be able to provide some on-track tuition and coaching to help you prepare for the test. By doing this, you will increase the chance of passing the test at the first attempt.

2.2 RACE LICENCES

The full rules and regulations concerning competition licences are contained within the current edition of the MSA Competitors Yearbook, known as the 'Blue Book'. This publication should be consulted at all times.

When you have successfully completed the NDTC course you can apply to the MSA for your first race licence. The application form should be sent, along with the appropriate fee, to the MSA and it will normally take around three weeks for the application to be processed and the licence returned. An express system is available at an additional fee for those drivers who need their licence within three working days.

All competition licences are valid until the end of the current year and so if you are granted a licence in the middle of the season, you will still need to renew it on January 1st for the following year.

There are two levels of National race licence, known as National A and National B. When you have passed the medical examination and completed your NDTC, you can apply for a National B licence. This will qualify you to race anywhere in the UK but you should remember that not all categories of racing are open to holders of National B licences. Typically, some of the classes for more powerful racing cars are only open to holders of a higher grade licence.

Anyone starting racing under a National B licence must display a novice cross on the back of the racing car until they have satisfactorily completed 10 races. This takes the form of a black cross on a yellow background and is a signal to other drivers that the bearer is a driver of limited circuit experience.

Progression from a National B to a National A licence requires the driver to show their capability over a minimum of 10 races. This is done by obtaining the signature of the Clerk of the Course on the reverse of the National B licence to record that that the driver has performed satisfactorily and finished the race without undue incident.

The minimum 10 signatures cannot all be obtained at the same race circuit and must not include more than five signatures from single-make

17

races using cars prepared or provided by the race organisers. A maximum of two signatures can be obtained at one meeting. To qualify for a licence signature, the driver needs to present his licence to the race officials when signing-on at the start of the meeting.

RACING LICENCES

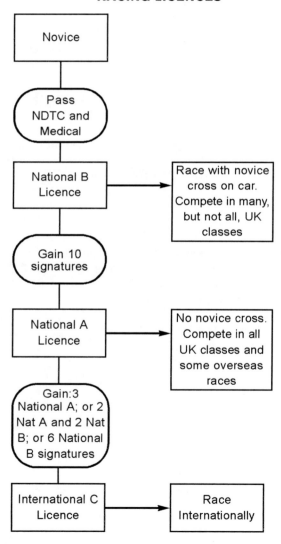

See Chapter 4.3

If the driver has performed satisfactorily, he or she will then be able to collect their licence after the race with another signature on the reverse. However, don't forget that there is a statutory 30-minute period after the provisional race results are published during which competitors have the right to protest the results. Licences will not be released until that 30-minute period has ended.

A driver who completes a day on a marshals' post during a race meeting can gain a signature from the CoC for that experience. This can be counted as an upgrading signature on their National B licence.

If a driver has ambitions to progress into international events, a similar upgrading process is necessary to move from a National A licence to an International C licence. The requirement is for signatures from three National A level events; or two national A plus two from National B level events; or six National B events. In all cases, signatures must be obtained at three different venues. There are separate requirements for drivers wishing to apply for the International Historic licence. For those competing at the very highest level of the sport there are two further grades of International licence.

However, for most drivers wishing to compete in Britain, a National A licence is sufficient. It is also worth noting that the higher grade licences attract a higher annual fee!

The 2000 licence fees were as follows:

National B	£38.50
National A	£56.50
International C	£105
International B	£182.50
International A	£558
International Historic	£105

It cannot be stressed too much just how important your race licence is. If you fail to produce your licence when signing-on for a race meeting, you face a fine or exclusion from the meeting. Further, all licences must be signed by the holder and have a passport size photograph of the holder permanently attached. Failure to have a photograph attached may lead to the licence being rejected by race officials.

Consider trying to find a passport photo booth close to Mallory Park on a wet Sunday morning in March..... If you are going to go racing, you need to keep the paperwork in order!

In just the same way that you can have your road licence endorsed or withdrawn, so penalties can be applied to your racing licence. If your on-track (and, indeed, off-track) conduct is considered inappropriate, your racing licence can be endorsed or withdrawn by the power of the officials of the meeting.

Breaches of the rules and regulations whilst competing can be punished by endorsement. Three such penalties will lead to a ban from racing for a period of time that can range from 30 days to many years. It should also be remembered that your conduct out of the car can come under scrutiny.

One sure-fire way of losing your racing licence is to follow up an on-track incident with a physical confrontation in the paddock after the race. A number of drivers have lost their licences for such incidents. In some cases, they have been banned from racing for five years.....

Finally, if you should be disqualified from driving on the road for some reason, it is not now necessary to advise the MSA. However, the MSA does retain the right to act against a driver who loses his or her road licence in a manner which is deemed to bring the sport into disrepute.

2.3 MEDICALS

The full rules and regulations concerning medicals are contained within the current edition of the MSA Competitors Yearbook, known as the 'Blue Book'. This publication should be consulted at all times.

ARE YOU SURE
YOU WANT TO
BE A RACING
DRIVER?

FOLEY

MEDICALS

All first-time applicants for race licences must pass a medical examination by their doctor before applying for their licence. After the first year, they will not then need a medical examination until the age of 45, although a medical self-declaration is required annually. International licence holders must, however, pass a medical examination each year. A fee (usually at least £40) will normally be charged by the doctor for the examination and must be paid directly to the doctor at the time.

The medical is similar to that which is carried out for life assurance assessment, but with specific attention to conditions such as diabetes, epilepsy and heart conditions. In such cases, a separate examination and review by the MSA Medical Consultant may be required. Eyesight is also checked and, of course, glasses or contact lenses are permitted.

It is now possible for disabled drivers to obtain a race licence although each case is considered on merit. Any potential applicant should contact the British Motor Sports Association for the Disabled in the first instance for specific advice.

See Chapter 8.3

2.4 BUYING RACEWEAR

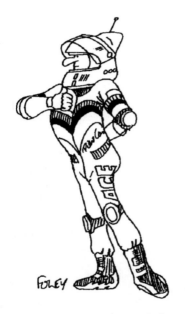

FOLEY

BUYING RACEWEAR

The full rules and regulations concerning race wear and helmets are contained within the current edition of the MSA Competitors Yearbook, known as the 'Blue Book'. This publication should be consulted at all times.

The next step on the journey towards your first race is to buy the mandatory fire resistant clothing and crash helmet. The MSA publishes information in the 'Blue Book' about the standard of equipment required and the minimum for clothing is a clean set of flame-resistant overalls.

The overalls should be manufactured from Nomex 111, Proban or equivalent materials. It is important to ensure that the overalls comply with the appropriate British standard as this will be checked by the scrutineers before the start of the meeting and you will not be permitted to use overalls that do not comply. The current acceptable standards are:

BS6249 part 1 Index A or B (but not C)
BSEN 533 or pr EN533 - 1995 Index 3;

Also, overalls bearing the FIA logo stitched into the fabric of the garment or on a sewn-in label are acceptable. If you are buying overalls for the first time, there is a wide range of styles and standards to suit all pockets. The cheapest overalls that meet the relevant standard can be bought for around £100. However, if you can afford a more expensive suit it will be a good investment. The best advice is to buy from a well-known outlet and seek advice from knowledgeable staff about what is best for you.

Drivers are strongly advised to wear flame resistant gloves, socks, balaclavas and underwear. Specially manufactured racing boots are also a good investment. On a practical note, overalls and boots will last longer if treated with care. If you work on your own car at race meetings, and most people do, it is always worth changing out of your racesuit and into some mechanics overalls before getting underneath to fix that oil leak.

Of course, the oil leak might just be caused by a piston-shaped hole in the side of the engine block, but there is no point in wrecking a good racesuit at the same time. If the wife/partner/lover/ etc. is kind, they may also offer to wash your racesuit from time to time. Take special care to follow the instructions as they are made of rather different materials.

Crash helmets must also meet the standard specified by the MSA and, once more, it is wise to buy the best crash helmet that your budget will stretch to. Along with your overalls, your crash helmet must be presented to the scrutineers when the car is checked before the meeting and they will be checking for obvious signs of damage as well as the required approval stickers.

The fit of a crash helmet is critical and it should be neither too tight or too loose. A helmet should be as closely-fitting as possible whilst still being comfortable. Take specialist advice when buying a helmet and take time to find the right size for you. Contrary to what is often said of racing drivers, the head is valuable and worth protecting. If you are unlucky enough to have an accident and bang your head, don't be surprised if the officials confiscate your crash helmet.

Though there may be no obvious external signs of damage, modern crash helmets are designed so that, in the case of a severe blow, the helmet will partially absorb the impact. In such a case, the event scrutineers are empowered to impound any helmet they consider no longer safe for use. If this happens, rather than feel aggrieved at the cost of replacing your helmet, feel thankful that it did the job it was designed to do. Crash helmets are only impounded for the safety of the driver concerned.

For your own safety, look after your crash helmet. If you ever drop it, you must, at the very least, return it to the manufacturer for proper inspection. Damage may not be readily apparent.

Currently, the acceptable helmet standards are:

BS 6658 - 85 A* (Type B is not acceptable)
BS 6658 Type A/FR
Snell SA2000
Snell SA95
SFI Foundation 31.1, 31.2
* No longer acceptable at International events.

Helmets must also carry a fluorescent yellow MSA approval sticker. Check this with the supplier before making your purchase. These standards are regularly reviewed and updated and older standards may become no longer acceptable. If your helmet goes out of date there is no choice but to buy a new one.

A soft bag to carry your helmet in is a good idea, as this will help keep it clean and free from scratches. Some people even retain the box that the helmet came in when new as a useful place to store it safely. Your crash helmet will be a major element of your initial spend so it is important to look after it properly. Only clean it with soap and water and read the manufacturer's instructions before putting any stickers on it.

You will see some wonderful helmet designs, particularly in Grand Prix racing. However, don't try and do something yourself, as some types of paint could be harmful to the helmet. If you want a smart design or your sponsors colours on your helmet, go to one of the specialist helmet painters who will know exactly what to do and, importantly, what not to do!

2.5 RACING SCHOLARSHIPS

RACING SCHOLARSHIPS

Over the years, there have been many scholarships aimed at helping ambitious drivers on their way up the racing ladder. Many have been well-conceived and provided valuable opportunities that have boosted careers. Some have fallen rather flat and a few have proved to be out and out confidence tricks. Thankfully, the latter type are few and far between but it is worth sounding a cautionary note, for some hopefuls have certainly been ripped off in the past.

At the top of the tree as far as ambitious young drivers are concerned is the BRDC/McLaren/Autosport Young Driver of the Year Award. This annual award to a promising young British driver was created in 1989 and has brought prestige, recognition, opportunity and financial backing for all of the winners. With three such prestigious organisations behind the award, it is a sure winner and all talented young drivers hope to win the award. However, it is solely aimed at those who have already proved themselves winners in one of the junior single-seater categories and is, therefore, out of the reach of the hopeful newcomer.

So how should you go about deciding to get involved in a scholarship? Well, the first thing to consider is the pedigree of the organisation running the award. How long has it been around, how many previous winners have there been and how did they fare? If the scheme involves parting with money in advance of the event, proceed with caution. Rather than rush ahead and send off your cash, stop and consider the value of the prize and likely response that would be needed to support such a prize.

25

A scholarship that promises a fully-funded season of racing in, for instance, Formula Ford, is going to have to raise a minimum income of around £50,000 before the organisers have even covered the cost of the award. Simply ask the question - does it add up?

However, there is one way of ensuring that you get value for money and a real chance of winning a real scholarship. A number of the ARDS-recognised racing schools run scholarships for promising pupils. Generally these are aimed at the most promising pupils and are a genuine opportunity for someone to progress their career at a very early stage. By dealing with an ARDS school you are assured proper technical back-up and your guarantee is the established reputation of the school.

Some of these scholarships will have an entry fee, but if you check what you will actually receive in terms of track time and tuition for your entry fee, you will find them good value even if you are not fortunate enough to win one of the prizes. And, by selecting an ARDS-school scholarship, you are assured a high standard of tuition and equipment.

2.6 INSURANCE

Just like anything in life, you can insure your racing car as well as ancillary equipment like trailers, tools, spares and garage equipment. As you might expect, the premiums for a racing car on the track are going to be rather more than your father pays for 2000 miles a year in his 1973 Austin Princess. But it is an expense worth investigating, even though it is not compulsory to have insurance for your racing car when it is being driven on the circuit.

As is the case in road car insurance, many different factors are involved in the calculation of premiums. The type of car, category, drivers' experience and number of races all have an effect on the premium. As an indication, a ten-year old Formula Ford 1600 with a total value of around £6000 would typically attract a premium in the region of £150 to £200 per race.

This is likely to be a deterrent to insurance for many drivers, but it is well worth considering if the car is hired or owned by a sponsor. Equally, if you are committed to a programme with a major sponsor that depends upon the car being ready for an agreed calendar of races, insurance may be prudent to ensure that you can meet your commitment.

Even if you decide that on-track insurance is not appropriate, there are other levels of vehicle insurance that may prove sensible. Cover can be arranged for the car when it is garaged and when it is in transit to and from the circuit. That same Formula Ford and trailer could be covered in this way for 12 months for around £150. Further, if most drivers worked out the value of tools and spares they have stashed away in their garage, they would probably be very surprised. Policies are available to cover this equipment.

Finally, the driver themselves really ought to be properly insured. Of course, you may be covered through other existing policies but before starting racing it is advisable to inform current insurers that you are participating in motor sport. The majority of life insurance companies will exclude motorsport unless it was accepted at the outset, but it is well worth checking as different companies exclude different levels of motorsport. If they do accept motorsport, seek that confirmation in writing!

Once again, there is no requirement to have any insurance cover and a small amount is automatically provided to all competition licence holders. It is important at this stage to take proper advice about your liabilities and then arrange cover accordingly. If your existing policies exclude motor racing, it is quite easy to arrange a specific or top up policy through one of the specialist motor sport insurers.

This is often a badly-neglected area but is worthy of very careful consideration. For instance, a married man in his 40s with a wife, two children and a mortgage, should be looking for up to £500,000 in life cover. Obviously, a 17 year-old with no dependants may not need anything like as much cover, but the cost of living with permanent injury following a serious accident should not be discounted. Packages can be tailored to suit individual needs and further investigation is strongly encouraged.

Two other areas of insurance should also be covered. If you are racing or testing on a licensed track or training with an **ARDS**-recognised school, public liability cover should be automatically provided by the organisers of that activity. However, if you make private arrangements to test your racing car at a local airfield for instance, you will have no such cover. Finally, if your racing team grows in size and becomes more professional, it may be worth considering a small business policy.

2.7 THE OFFICIALS OF THE MEETING

THE RACING OFFICIALS

Contrary to what some drivers may feel at times, the officials of the meeting are there to ensure the meeting runs smoothly, safely and in accordance to the relevant rules and regulations. They are not simply there to make life difficult for drivers!

Before we go any further on this subject, there is something very important to be said, something that most drivers seem to forget at some point. Virtually every official in motor racing you will come into contact with is a volunteer giving up his or her time so that you can race. At best, they will be receiving modest expenses. They love the sport as much as you do, perhaps more.

Starting from the top is the 'headmaster' for the day, the Clerk of the Course. He is top dog and if you are called to see him, it is unlikely that he wishes to congratulate you on a particularly fine piece of driving! The CoC is responsible for the overall safe conduct of the meeting and is usually the first point of call for drivers who have committed some misdemeanour.

OFFICIALS AT A RACE MEETING

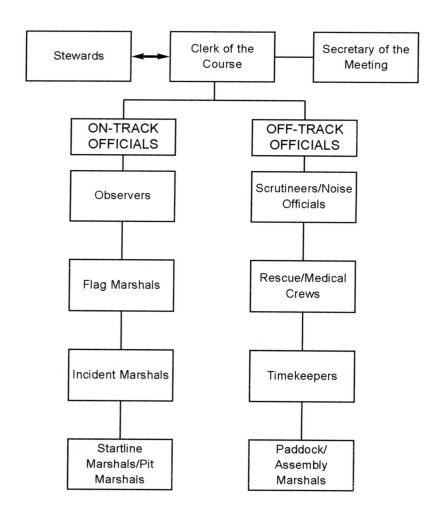

By the very nature of the job, the CoC carries considerable authority and is often called upon to make tough decisions on a whole range of subjects, including imposing penalties on drivers, when to stop races, track and weather conditions and many more. It is probable that, if called to see the CoC after qualifying or a race, he will be acting upon a report received from one of his observers.

These senior marshals are stationed around the track, and as well as being responsible for a team of marshals, will also be reporting back to race control (the nerve centre of the race meeting) about what drivers are getting up to. Be warned: Clerks of the Course have heard just about every excuse in the book before, so if you are guilty of a misdemeanour, you're better off taking it on the chin!

The CoC is also the judicial body for dealing with any protests raised by competitors. He has the power to penalise or exclude drivers, impose fines and withhold upgrading signatures on competition licences where he sees fit.

Should a driver appeal against any such penalty, this will then be heard by the Stewards of the Meeting. At race meetings there will be three Stewards, one of them appointed by the MSA. The Stewards have no involvement in the running of the meeting and are the second judicial body at a race meeting. They will hear and adjudicate on any appeal against a decision of the CoC. The Stewards will also report on the running of the meeting to the MSA.

Working closely with the CoC is the Secretary of the Meeting, who will often be the first point of contact for competitors. The Secretary will handle the administration of the meeting, including receiving entries, organising competitors signing-on and look after a hundred and one other things.

All competitors will come into contact with the event scrutineers, who fall into two distinct categories. Before the start of practice, competitors are required to present their car for scrutineering when the basic safety of the vehicle will be checked along with the drivers' helmet and overalls.

See Chapter 4.3

Some race meetings, particularly, of a higher status, will also have eligibility scrutineers on duty. Typically, these officials will be appointed to specific championships to check the compliance with the rules of the competing cars. They have the power to measure components, strip certain components and apply and remove seals on controlled items. Often, the eligibility scrutineer will examine successful cars at the end of the race to check compliance with the rules.

Working in conjunction with the scrutineers, and becoming ever-more important, is the environmental scrutineer. This is the man with the noise meter and his role is crucial. The noise levels generated by competing cars will normally be checked prior to the start of qualifying and may be monitored during qualifying and the race.

The need to make the sport as environmentally friendly as possible is a pressing issue and noise testing is becoming more vigorous each year. In recent seasons, there have been several instances of race leaders being black-flagged (called into the pits) due to their cars recording excessive readings on noise meters. The silencing system on a race car must be carefully prepared and maintained in good condition.

Out on the track, aside from the observers, are teams of flag marshals and incident marshals. The flag marshals are there to communicate information to the drivers via a range of coloured flags. The colours of the flags and their meanings will have been covered in preparation for the Novice Driver Training Course. Drivers who fail to respond to these flags put themselves and their fellow racers in danger and, at the least, could find themselves up before the CoC with some serious explaining to do!

See Chapter 8.5

The incident marshals are the people you least want to come into contact with. That's not because they aren't nice people... They will be the guys (and girls) who descend upon you should you be unlucky enough to fall off. You may be upset at having just parked the results of months of labour in the tyre wall, but it wasn't their fault, so don't take out your frustrations on them. Their priorities are to deal with any fires (thankfully very rare) and then get you to a position of safety and your car as far out of harm's way as possible.

Also, should your pride and joy fail to last the distance, the incident marshals will get you parked as safely as possible. Here, a word of warning. You may think you can coax an ailing motor car back to the pits but if you are caught on the racing line when the battling leaders come over the brow, you could have serious problems.

Far better, if the car is failing, to pull off in good time where you can guide the car well clear of the track and into a position of safety at the direction of the marshals. Too often, cars have drifted to a halt in a position that puts the driver in danger, the marshals in danger having to move it and the other drivers in danger as they dodge around it. If in doubt, park it sooner rather than later. The recovery crews don't charge for towing you back to the paddock after the race!

Don Truman, legendary Clerk of the Course at Mallory Park, often has a succinct way of covering this during his drivers briefings: 'If you park it, some other bugger will find it!' Consider the fact that previously undamaged cars left in foolish positions have, moments later, been written off by an out-of-control rival.

There are many other race officials who perform vital but often unseen roles. The timekeepers, medical and rescue staff, pit, paddock and startline marshals are all there working away behind the scenes. In all dealings with officials, be courteous and professional and you shouldn't go far wrong! If you want to know more about marshalling, contact the British Motor Racing Marshals' Club.

See Chapter 8.3

CHAPTER 3
SO NOW YOU HAVE A LICENCE

IN THIS CHAPTER

3.1 CHOOSING A CATEGORY
- ➤ The major race organisers
- ➤ The diversity of British racing
- ➤ What does it all cost?
- ➤ How to choose a category

3.2 D-I-Y OR PROFESSIONAL TEAM?
- ➤ Buying or hiring a car
- ➤ The likely costs
- ➤ Professional teams
- ➤ Where to find a car

3.3 BUYING A RACING CAR
- ➤ Making the right choice
- ➤ Negotiating to buy a car
- ➤ What to look out for
- ➤ Converting a road car

3.4 CAR PREPARATION
- ➤ Making it safe and legal
- ➤ Checking the basics

3.5   TESTING
> The importance of testing
> When and where to test
> Planning the test day
> Setting targets

3.6   MENTAL AND PHYSICAL PREPARATION FOR THE DRIVER
> The physical and mental challenge
> In the 'office'
> Food and drink before the event and on race day
> Personal fitness

3.7   DRIVER COACHING
> The benefits of coaching
> The ARDS-instructor as a coach

3.1 CHOOSING A CATEGORY

Four motor racing clubs organise a major proportion of the race meetings in Britain. The British Racing Drivers' Club - which owns Silverstone; and the British Automobile Racing Club - which operates the Thruxton circuit in Hampshire and the Welsh Motor Sports Centre at Pembrey in South Wales, both run circuits as well as organising race meetings.

The British Racing and Sports Car Club, meanwhile, is the most active race-organising club in the world with an annual programme of more than 70 race meetings. Finally, the 750 Motor Club organises race meetings at most UK venues and specialises in low-cost racing for a wide variety of cars.

Many other clubs also run race meetings, some of them just once a year. The Historic Sports Car Club specialises in events for single-seater, sports cars and saloon cars from the 1950s, 60s and 70s. Racing for Pre-War cars is still very popular and the Vintage Sports Car Club caters for those with a love of older cars.

This wide diversity is an important aspect of British motor racing. If you have a car, there is somewhere to race it! Over 140 championships or series of races are held each year for just about every conceivable type of car. From a Citroen 2CV to a year-old Formula 1 car, there is a class of racing in Britain that caters for them!

See Chapter 7

Racing categories can be broadly split into three groups. Single-seater racing cars are, in effect, scaled down Grand Prix cars with a semi-prone driving position and exposed wheels. Saloon cars and sports cars come in all shapes, sizes and ages, while sports cars can be either open or closed.

So just how much does it all cost? There is no simple answer to this question. However, it is certainly true to say that it does not need to cost as much as many people first think.

The British amateur racing scene is far removed from the multi-million pound world of Grand Prix racing. At the top level in this country, the sport is certainly not cheap. The Touring Car teams are likely to spend around a million pounds per car per season. A full budget to contest a season in the British Formula 3 Championship is now around £350,000.

However, these budgets only apply to a very small number of the 5000 people who go racing in Britain each year, many of whom race competitively on very limited resources. If you have £5000 you can most certainly get started in racing, less in some classes.

Before you reach the grid for your first race, there are several areas of expenditure that cannot be avoided. Earlier we mentioned the steps towards gaining a racing licence. These will cost around £200 in the first year but will be less than £100 in subsequent seasons. Membership of one of the race-organising clubs is also essential and the choice of club will be determined by the class of racing you are aiming at. Each category is allied to one of the major organising clubs and racing membership will cost around £80 a year.

The choice of which category to enter is one of the most difficult decisions to make. The best way of making the correct choice is to spend some time researching the classes available. A few Sundays spent at race meetings will be a good investment. By watching the different classes and visiting the paddock, you will get a good feel for what each class is about.

You will find most amateur drivers very approachable and their comments will give pointers to which class is right for you. Most championships have a co-ordinator who can supply more information about the class and the likely costs involved. By taking some time to get a feel for the sport before making a choice, prospective racers can save themselves making the wrong decision.

See Chapter 3.3

3.2   D-I-Y OR PROFESSIONAL TEAM?

Once you have made your choice of category, there is another important decision to be made. Do you prepare and maintain your own car, or do you have this work done professionally? This decision will really depend upon your resources, in terms of time, money and technical ability.

There are many classes of racing where you will be able to do much, if not all, of the work yourself. If you have a reasonable mechanical understanding, or have friends with that ability, it is relatively easy to run a car yourself. Most racing cars are easier to work on than a standard road car because they are designed for one purpose.

If you don't have too much money, concentrate on getting a good car and running it yourself. You will probably be surprised at how low the cost of going racing can be. It really does not need to cost telephone number budgets. If you do run the car yourself, you will learn a great deal about the mechanics of the car.

For instance, you could buy a reasonable Formula Ford 1600 for between £3000 and £5000 and, barring accident damage or major engine failures, spend the same again contesting a season of 12 races if you run the car yourself. It may sound obvious, but it is important to discipline yourself not to crash! If you are going out trying to win races and are crashing all the time, you will never make any progress.

However, if you are short on mechanical knowledge, you may need to have some or all of the work done professionally. The cost of this work really depends upon the type of car you intend to race. In some of the professional categories, there are a selection of teams who will look after everything. You simply arrive at the race meeting and drive the car. However, this will probably cost a minimum of £20,000 per season in one of the higher-profile classes, and rises into six figures at the very top of the British racing ladder.

Further down the racing ladder, there are racing teams who will supply a race-prepared car for as little as £500 per race in the amateur classes. A full season, typically consisting of 12 races, could cost as little as £6000. In this type of arrangement, the team would retain ownership of the car and the customer would be responsible for the cost of any damage. Racing cars can be insured but, of course, the premiums are higher than those for road cars.

See Chapter 2.6

By far the most popular route for amateur racers is to buy their own racing car and prepare and maintain it themselves in their spare time. Often, friends and family become involved, both before the races and during the event by acting as pit crew and helpers.

In these amateur classes, which include single-seaters, sports cars and saloon cars, complete second-hand race cars can be bought for well under £5000. If the car is then maintained to a good standard, it will lose little of its value during the season. Indeed, if you buy a car and are successful with it or improve its standard of preparation, you can even add to its value during the course of the year.

The best places to find details of cars for sale are in the classified pages of the two weekly motor sport magazines, Autosport and Motoring News, and the monthly title Cars and Car Conversions. All are essential reading for prospective racers and a vital source of cars and equipment. And if you do well in the races, you will be able to read about yourself!

Once the initial purchase is made, running costs for a season in one of the amateur classes should be no more than £5000. The major elements in this cost are event entry fees, fuel (for both the race car and the vehicle to tow the trailer), tyres and general maintenance. Don't forget that the

Go Racing?
Yes You Can!

...se are just two of the 12
...o Motorsport Championships
...by the 750 Motor Club
...ng 2001 -
...meetings at the leading UK
...e circuits.

HOT/STOCK HATCH

Membership benefits
include discounts
across a wide range
of parts and services
plus free monthly
magazine.

...MULA 750

...the
...best
...ow cost,
...ry-level
...orsport....

For further details call:
Robin Knight, Competition Secretary
01379 384 268 or fax 01379 384 055

or

Neil Carr-Jones, Membership Secretary
01825 750 760 or fax 01825 750 566
750 Motor Club, Worth Farm, Little Horsted,
East Sussex, TN22 5TT

tyres and brakes will work much harder on the race track than on the road and will, therefore, wear out much sooner.

Engine and gearbox maintenance need to be considered as racing places a much greater strain on these components. However, barring a disaster, such as an accident or engine blow-up, £5000 in running costs should see you through a season of racing in one of the classes recognised as a starter class. Typically, the best ones to consider are those for road-going saloons or sports cars, where there is a natural limit to costs.

There really is a category to suit every pocket. It is far better to start off in a relatively lowly class and work your way up as you learn, rather than come in at too high a level and end up broke and disillusioned.

However, there is another way to avoid making the wrong decision early in your racing career. Some of the ARDS-recognised racing schools offer pupils the opportunity to race with the school. In some cases, this takes the form of dedicated school races against fellow pupils. Although run under the control of the school, these races are genuine events run under an MSA permit and a driver can gain upgrading signatures for satisfactory performance. These races count towards proper championships, and the successful drivers may find subsequent opportunities within scholarships run by the school. By taking part in these events, drivers can try the sport out for a limited out-lay and experience proper racing while remaining under the coaching and guidance of the school and the instructors.

Alternatively, several schools run their own racing teams where suitable pupils can arrange to hire cars for one or more races in various categories (usually single-seaters). For a fixed fee, the school team will prepare the car, take it to the circuit and oversee the race, offering encouragement and support for the novice racer. A first race can be a pretty daunting occasion, and having the experience of the school behind you should make the day far more enjoyable. For good advice on racing within the framework of a racing school, speak to one of the senior instructors for more information.

3.3   Buying a racing car

FOR SALE
GOOD TYRES
NICE SEAT
NEW HEAD
REST

FOLEY

BUYING A CAR

Car preparation really starts before you've even bought the car. The best advice is to go to a number of race meetings and start having a look around at the type of categories that appeal to you. Then, when you've identified the category you want to race in and sorted out how much money you can afford to spend, go and talk to as many competitors in that class as possible.

This will give you background information about the various cars and will help you build up a picture about which are the sensible cars to look at and which are the cars you really don't want to buy. This will also help you build up information on the history of the cars that are available. But always bear in mind that some views may be biased!

Another valuable source of information is from the club that organises the particular championship you have chosen. All championships have a co-ordinator and they are usually a good source of un-biased information.

When you are at race meetings looking at the options, take time to go and speak to the event scrutineers. Go to the meeting early and watch the pre-race scrutineering going on. This will give you useful pointers as to what the officials are looking for when they make the mandatory safety checks on each car. During the middle of the day when there is not a queue of cars waiting to be checked, seek out one of the scrutineers and tell them of your plans.

They will normally be happy to share some of their knowledge about what to look out for from a safety and scrutineering point of view when buying a car. They may well fill you in on things that are specific to the type of car you are looking at, because they will have been looking in detail at the cars. They may be aware of specific weaknesses or problems that may be typical of the car, and then when you go to look at cars, you can be alert to this.

Although they rightly carry considerable powers during a race meeting, scrutineers are enthusiasts who volunteer their time and effort for little reward. Providing you pick a sensible time to approach them and explain your situation, you should gain benefit from their knowledge.

When you do start negotiating to buy a car, talk to the seller about how much help they can provide initially when you purchase the car. Quite often, if someone is selling a car they are either giving up racing completely or moving to another category. If so, they are more likely to help you with all the information you need about running the car. In motorsport, everyone who takes part is enthusiastic about the sport, so try and use that enthusiasm to your advantage!

There is a lot of free advice out there and before anybody puts their money down on a car, they must try to contain their enthusiasm. Most people can't wait to get started and rush out and buy a car, without knowing what its all about. Then they waste the first year resolving problems that could have been avoided with proper research and a degree of patience! The best advice is; don't rush in.

The more ground work you do, the more successful you will be and the more fun you will have when you first start. Make sure you take a look at a number of cars before making any decision. This will help you build up knowledge of the market and ensure that you ultimately make a good choice. Second-hand racing cars is invariably a buyer's market, so use that to your advantage.

When you decide how much to spend on a car, make sure you leave enough room in your budget to actually be able to run the car in races. Even the basics like fuel, tyres and entry fees need to be paid for out of your precious reserves.

If you are going to buy a competitive car, where its price will almost certainly be enhanced by its pedigree, try and arrange to load it onto your trailer at the end of its last race with its current owner. Too often, a winning car has returned to its base before collection by the proud new purchaser and lost some of the best bits and pieces in the process! Stories of different engines being fitted before sale are sadly quite common, so try and protect against this.

This is particularly a risk if the seller is staying in the same category but moving to a new, or newer, car. If the seller is changing course, it is less likely that the car you see do well in its last race will be dramatically different to the car you collect two weeks later. Also, if the current owner is moving on, there is every chance that a spares package will be included as part of the deal.

If someone has raced a car for a couple of seasons, it is inevitable that they will have built up their own spares package. Motor racing is always a buyer's market, and use your strong position to extract the best deal available to you on spares and things like wheels and tyres.

The first thing to look at when inspecting a car is how clean is it? That will actually be a good indication of how well prepared the car is. If the car is dirty and has got grease and oil all over it, then the odds are that the standard of preparation will be quite poor and that things like rose joints haven't been replaced for a long time. These are the type of things that can fail and end up costing you a lot of money.

If a car is really clean and well presented, as racing cars should always be, then you at least know that the owner has been paying some attention to it. Even if they have only just cleaned the car up to sell it!

Also, if the car is clean and is a single-seater, you will be able to get all the bodywork off and look to see if there are any obvious cracks in the chassis. If you are not familiar with the type of car you are going to look at, take someone with you who is. Even if you know what you are looking for, it is always better to have two pairs of eyes looking at a car.

45

If you are there to buy your first racing car, you are going to be led by your heart and be thinking, 'I've got to have it!' If you take someone with you who is slightly removed from that desire, they can prove to be a worthwhile calming influence.

Nowadays, there are a number of classes where a road car can be modified for racing at modest expense and you may consider either converting a car you already own, or buying a standard car with the express intention of racing it. If you take this route, the main requirement is to locate a car that is structurally sound. Cars that have suffered cosmetic accident damage or have been stolen and recovered can provide a good base for a competition car and will be more likely to be priced attractively.

Also, higher mileage cars may not be a bad buy, particularly if you intend to have the engine and gearbox re-worked before you go racing. From then on, much of the work needed will be to meet the required safety standards for things like roll cages, seats, harnesses, external electrical cut-out switches and fire extinguisher systems. All of this is covered in detail in Section Q of the 'Blue Book' and it is essential that you study this carefully before embarking upon a project! Make sure that the relevant controls are properly marked as designated in the Blue Book. If you don't do this, the scrutineers will almost certainly pull you up at your first meeting.

The most popular classes for road-going saloons are those for Road Saloons, Hot Hatches and Stock Hatches. If this is where you decide to start racing, look at what are the most popular models for these championships and, ideally, go with the trend. Not only will you find more drivers at meetings able to offer advice and assistance, but the supply of competition parts for the more popular cars will be much better.

See Chapter 7

3.4 CAR PREPARATION

CAR PREPARATION

The first aim of race car preparation should always be to ensure conformity with the safety and technical regulations specified in the MSA Blue Book and the relevant championship regulations. The latter document will clearly state what can be done to the car. If the regulations don't specifically say that something can be done, it probably can't! In all cases, follow these two documents as your bibles. Some of the following text may not be appropriate to all classes of racing - only a careful study of the technical regulations will identify just what is permitted.

The most important aspect of race car preparation is to check, check and check again. There is simply no substitute for checking everything that can be checked as frequently as possible. The use of a printed check-list of items to be covered between races can be a good way of keeping on top of the situation, and ensuring that nothing vital is over-looked.

The major difference between a road car and a race car is that a race car is, theoretically, driven on the limit all the time and so all of the components will have a much shorter life. It is very easy to under-estimate this so you need to be very aware of the stresses that are being put on components and cover all the basic things when looking at, and indeed preparing the car.

Basic preparation will cover essential safety items like wheel bearings, brakes, steering and suspension. Brakes should be a number one priority when preparing the car and make sure you bleed the system properly. Find out exactly what grade of brake fluid you should be using for the particular car, make sure the fluid is always fresh and replace it regularly. Check the brake seals regularly. One of the most likely modifications, even in the classes for road-going cars, will be to improve the brakes.

The first step may be as simple as fitting competition brake pads as the standard items will be unlikely to stand the pressure of racing. The regulations for the class you have chosen will detail what else can, or cannot, be done in terms of up-rating brakes. Bigger calipers and discs are a sensible modification if permitted and a better set of discs is very worthwhile. Competition discs will typically be grooved to allow better heat dissipation and will be made of better material than the standard item.

When you have bought a car, pay particular attention to the tyres. In many classes, you will be restricted to one particular make of tyre and, if this is the case, talk to the tyre supplier and get some tyre information. If the tyres on the car have been stood for any appreciable amount of time, throw them away and replace them. This may sound an expensive move, but it will be nothing like as expensive as the likely outcome of a tyre failure during a race.

Suspension modifications will, once again, be controlled by the class regulations. However, in the case of a road car modified for racing, the aim is to be as low and stiff as possible, with due regard to minimum ride heights. The best way to start is by replacing any rubber bushes in the suspension with, if permitted, urethane or nylon bushes. This will sharpen the car considerably if it has road origins.

Good car preparation is all about attention to detail. You need to put the time and effort in and, if necessary, you may need to get help from other sources. Good preparation is not necessarily about spending money, either. Time is the critical factor.

If you have just bought your first racing car, allow yourself plenty of time to prepare it. Do not be tempted to rush into your first race because if you are not properly prepared, you may well end up wasting a lot of time and money.

3.5 TESTING

Before the first race, try and give the car a number of runs in test sessions. That way, you can locate any potential faults on the car at a time when you are not under pressure to complete a race. Inevitably, when you do start racing, you will want to at least finish the race and start getting signatures on your racing licence.

During a test session, you can go out and do a couple of laps and if you're not sure about something on the car, you can come back into the pits and sort it out. Equally, as the driver, you can build yourself up gradually as you explore the car's capabilities away from the pressure of a race meeting.

Just as you should give yourself plenty of time when looking around to buy a car, do the same as you prepare towards your first race. Allow ample time to work through the car before the first test and then allow more time to carry out some testing before you plan to race it for the first time. It may be worthwhile, even before you select the car, to sit down and make a timetable to plan what you are going to do at what stage.

Just how long the various stages of preparation will take can vary enormously depending on the type of car you plan to race, what knowledge you have and what resources are available to you. But the thing that drivers invariably find is that they run out of time as the first scheduled race draws near. Going into your first race ill-prepared will invariably lead to disappointment or, perhaps, much worse.

An old adage that holds good in this situation is that if you are failing to plan, you are planning to fail. Setting yourself sensible targets and then keeping to them will add professionalism to your racing and, ultimately help make it more enjoyable and, hopefully, more successful.

Before a test day, sit down and work out a plan for the entire day of what you are going to do and what you hope to achieve. During the day, you may have to revise the plan, but at least at the start of the day you know what you are trying to achieve. This should ensure that you are covering specific areas and are not just working on a hit and miss basis. Testing does not come cheaply and it is important to make the best use of valuable track time.

See Chapter 8.2

Try and keep testing to short runs of perhaps three or four laps at a time. Then, come back to the pits and analyse what happened in those laps so that when you next go out, you have specific things that you are trying to achieve with your driving. And, of course, you may well want to spend some of the test day working on the set up of the car in areas like gear ratios, suspension settings and aerodynamic changes. Just what scope you have for change will, of course, depend largely upon the type of car your are racing.

However, in the early stages of your racing, you will be so busy with just driving the car that you will probably not be aware of all the other things that are going on around you. For instance, simply by changing gear ratios, you could find half a second per lap improvement immediately.

When you go testing, set yourself sensible targets. Before the test, try and speak to one of the instructors from the racing school based at the circuit. They will generally be very helpful with information about the racing line, the likely gearing needed for the car you are driving and any other relevant details. This will give you a base point to work from and could also save you pounding round and round, trying to figure out what to do and which gear to use. You should find most instructors quite willing to help out in this way. There is no point in trying to re-invent the wheel at this stage of your racing career!

Recently, a team spent over a year rebuilding a car after a substantial crash in readiness for a novice driver to start racing. They finally finished repairing the damage and went to Mallory Park to give the car a preliminary shakedown test before its first race. The novice driver went out in the car and tried much too hard too soon. On just his third lap of the test session, he made a mistake and crashed heavily, leaving the car even more badly damaged than it had been first time around.

The result: damage totalling many thousands of pounds, a disillusioned team and a driver who dropped out of the sport even before his first race. It is not a unique story, but could easily have been avoided with a steady build up for car and driver.

An added advantage of doing some testing before your first race is that you should have less of a culture shock when you then arrive for your first race. If you simply buy a car and turn up for your first race, you could be in for a big surprise.

It is not uncommon for a new driver to arrive for their first race with a mental picture of their own driving capabilities putting them somewhere in the middle of the field. However, they suddenly find that they are three seconds a lap slower than even the next slowest car in the race. Then, they've got a much bigger mountain to climb than if they'd taken time to prepare themselves and built up to a sensible speed before entering their first race.

By learning some of the ropes before the first race, you have a better chance of starting off in the middle of the pack. At least then the leaders will be in sight! Of course, not everyone who goes racing does it purely to win. In any race, there can only be one winner from, perhaps 30 cars. Other drivers race for the pleasure and excitement of doing it, and there is no disgrace in finishing further down the order. In every race, someone must finish last.

The target for your first race should, therefore, be to finish without being hopelessly out-classed by the rest of the field and not to do anything silly. Do not expect to win your first race. It may happen in your dreams, but is incredibly unlikely in reality.

If you draw a parallel with a sport like golf, you would not expect to buy a set of clubs, teach yourself how to use them, and then turn up at a competition and win, having never been round the course before. So why should anyone expect motor racing to be any different?

The problem with motor racing in this respect, is that everyone can drive a road car before they start racing. But the two activities are so far removed from each other that many people cannot believe the difference once they start racing. People who think they drive fast on the road are in for a big shock if they think racing will simply be an extension of that. There is a lot to learn and you can't learn it all in your first test session.

3.6 MENTAL AND PHYSICAL PREPARATION FOR THE DRIVER

Proper mental and physical preparation for the driver is vital to the outcome of the race. It can be the difference between winning and losing, or having a good race or a bad race. First of all, you need to be reasonably fit, depending upon the type of car you are planning to race. The medical examination before you gained your licence will have ensured a basic level of health. But what many drivers find tiring is the mental side of racing and the concentration that is needed.

When driving on a circuit, even after as little as three laps, you can feel very drained. Race driving demands a level of concentration that people are not used to. We all drive on the road in quite a relaxed fashion and seldom concentrate 100%. In a race car, there is nothing but pure concentration. That is what tires a lot of people.

Above and beyond that, is the actual stress of driving a racing car on a circuit and the pressure you put on yourself. The adrenalin is pumping and everyone finds it very tiring, especially in the early days of a racing career. You need to be able to build yourself up to that very gradually by doing some form of mental exercise to improve your levels of concentration.

Ultimately, you should be trying to develop the ability to overcome the emotion and stress of a racing situation and take a more clinical

VRMM...
VRRMM...

JIM

PREPARING PHYSICALLY

approach. This will help you perform to the best of your ability but is not a skill that is easily mastered. Many drivers suffer from inconsistent performances, one race battling for the lead and the next struggling in the midfield. Invariably, this is down to mental condition and concentration, rather than variations in car performance.

When you are driving quickly, it is important to be able to understand why that is the case and, conversely, when you are not going so well, be able to pinpoint what changes you need to make. In terms of physical preparation, it is strongly advisable not to drink alcohol at all in the lead up to a race. Ideally, allow plenty of time for any alcohol to completely clear out of your system. It is worth noting that the race officials are able to carry out random tests at a race meeting to check for any driver under the influence of alcohol or drugs.

Recently, a driver attended a barbecue on the Saturday evening before a race meeting and drank several pints of beer. The following morning he was selected for a random blood test and proved to still be over the specified limit. Not only was he excluded from the race meeting, but was fined and had his racing licence endorsed.

It is, of course, utter folly to attempt to race when under the influence of alcohol or drugs. You risk not only your own life, but those of your fellow competitors and race organisers will quite correctly come down very heavily on anyone transgressing. Equally, if you have invested time and effort in your racing car, you would not deliberately do something to hinder its performance. So, why do the same thing to the driver?

Take time to create the right driving position, for this is the office environment when you are racing. If you are not comfortable and in the correct position, your performance will suffer. The ideal driving position in a saloon or sportscar is to have the seat upright, with your shoulders supported and hands at the classic ten to two position.

Make sure you know where everything is in the cockpit and that you can reach all of the switches and controls and see all of the important instruments. If the first you know of falling oil pressure is when a piston pokes through the bonnet, you have just learnt an expensive lesson.

In the lead up to a race, you should try and spend some time focusing on what you will be doing on the day of the race. Part of that preparation should be to ensure that your body is in the best condition possible for the rigours of racing. During the race, particularly in warmer weather, you will lose body fluids and so you should stock up on suitable fluids accordingly. This will be particularly true for sports and saloon cars where heat can build up inside the cockpit.

The exact quantity to drink is very much down to the individual and you most certainly do not want to finish the race with your legs crossed having drunk too much liquid before the race! Trial and error is the best way, but you will find many drivers drinking copious amounts of mineral water immediately after the race. In endurance races it is common for cars to be fitted with some form of drinks bottle and a tube to the driver's helmet so that he can drink during the race.

Just as drinking alcohol can slow your reactions, so can excessive food. A sensible approach is to limit breakfast to cereals and toast. If you then have lunch between qualifying and the race on a one-day meeting, try and eat in plenty of time before the race so that your body has time to digest the food. The key is to plan the day and meals accordingly. If you are having particular problems, or want to take the matter further, it is best to seek professional advice.

The other thing that racing drivers should avoid the night before a race is sex! This will be more of a problem to some drivers than others and is best left to personal decision.....

The level of personal fitness required to race successfully will vary from class to class and in the entry-level classes, you need not be superfit to race successfully. However, regular exercise is beneficial to every day life as well as racing. Cardio-vascular exercise is always useful, as is any activity that helps increase your stamina. If you progress higher up the racing ladder, you will almost certainly need to work on fitness as upperbody and neck muscles will come under increasing strain as cornering speeds increase.

Top level drivers are among the fittest of all sportsmen. If you feel this is an area you could improve, you should consider working with a fitness trainer who is qualified to show you exercises that will suit your particular situation. Any local gym should be able to provide you with the name of a professional trainer.

3.7 DRIVER COACHING

The hardest thing for many drivers to admit, is that a lack of front-running speed may be down to the driver and not the car. The 'Racing Drivers Book of Excuses' is an oft-quoted mythical publication that, if ever written, would run to many hundreds of pages!

There are many ways of approaching your first race. A route chosen by some aspiring racers is to spend time at a racing school, building up their confidence and speed with tuition and one to one driver coaching. Then, when they arrive at their first race, they are on the pace straightaway and comfortable with their new surroundings.

This does not have to be the case, however, and there are a lucky few who have sufficient natural ability to be able to jump straight into a car and run competitively with little or no coaching. But, let's face it, they are the exception and not every driver is going to be the next Michael Schumacher. Indeed, many of them have no particular wish to be a Grand Prix star.

DRIVER COACHING

Others turn up for their first meeting without much of a clue about what they are doing and find that they are completely lost. They don't know their way around the track, don't know which gears to use and are a danger to themselves as well as the rest of the competitors. This is when personal frustration can set in. Equally, they can then waste a lot of money thinking that the scope for improvement must be in the chassis or the engine.

However, they should really be looking inside the cockpit for the source of the problem. Does the driver know what he is doing? If you are three seconds a lap off the pace at your first meeting, the chances are that those three seconds are in the driver and not the equipment.

The easiest way of proving this beyond doubt, is to have an experienced ARDS instructor come and drive your car as part of a coaching programme arranged through a racing school. If he is able to produce competitive times, you have a performance yardstick. Further, a good coach will highlight any areas of improvement in the car that will aid your performance even further.

Although there is inevitably a cost involved in enlisting the support of a driver coach, it could prove to be very cost-effective. Consider the alternatives. First, you invest more money in the equipment, perhaps an engine rebuild or some development work which may prove to be largely worthless. Second, in frustration at your relative lack of speed, you start trying too hard and run the risk of having an accident as you try and find the time you are losing.

Not everyone will use a coach, and we don't suggest that it is an essential step in the learning process. But, if you are struggling to match the pace of your rivals, time spent with a coach - who will probably charge between £150 and £200 per day - may just be the most cost-effective way of getting to the root of your problems. If you talk to any driver who has had proper professional coaching, they will rate the benefits very highly. One day with a good coach could teach you more than two seasons of racing.

Another time to consider coaching is when you feel you have reached a plateau in your own performance, and are not making any real forward progress. Of course, if you are now winning races by a considerable margin, it could be that there is no further room for improvement, but this is seldom the case!

A good coach should, in most cases, be able to help you move forward from that plateau to the next level of performance. It is fair to say that some very experienced drivers have faults to which they are oblivious. A number of Grand Prix drivers work with coaches and, if you consider a sport like tennis or golf, even the very best players in the world have coaches.

The professional coach will start with the preparation of the driver before they even get into the car. Properly fitting helmets and overalls may seem obvious, but ill-fitting race wear can affect performance. If you are racing a sports car or saloon car, it may be possible to arrange to fit a passenger seat so that the coach can sit alongside you and vice versa. If used with an intercom system, this can be even more effective, as it allows instant communication.

If you are driving a single-seater, the racing school may be able to provide a second car so that the coach can first lead you round and then follow you around to assess what you are doing and how to improve your performance. Being pulled round can be a very effective way of improving your driving and, importantly, your lap times.

Taking this a stage further, nowadays many cars are fitted with some form of data-logging system which records what is happening to the car on each lap in considerable detail. The analysis of this data has become a major part of the work of professional and semi-professional teams and drivers.

However, you need to be able to interpret the data you are gathering. It is now fashionable to have this equipment in racing cars but before you invest in the kit, make sure you have a way of understanding the data you are collecting! If you are inexperienced, you could end up confusing yourself.

See Chapter 5.5

If working with a driver coach who is also driving your car, you will then be able to overlay data and draw very specific conclusions about where and why you are losing time on the circuit.

CHAPTER 4
THE FIRST RACE MEETING

IN THIS CHAPTER

4.1 ENTERING YOUR FIRST RACE
- ➢ Club memberships
- ➢ Championship registration
- ➢ Entry forms

4.2 TESTING: WHEN WHERE AND HOW MUCH?
- ➢ How often to test
- ➢ Where to go testing
- ➢ Be prepared to travel
- ➢ Making the most of track time

4.3 THE FIRST RACE DAY
- ➢ Final instructions
- ➢ Planning the day
- ➢ The paperwork
- ➢ Signing-on
- ➢ Scrutineering

4.4 QUALIFYING
- ➢ How to plan the session
- ➢ The minimum requirements
- ➢ The first lap
- ➢ Setting a time
- ➢ The time sheets

4.5 PIT SIGNALS

- ➤ Where to signal from
- ➤ What information?
- ➤ In-car displays
- ➤ Signals in the race
- ➤ Getting in and out of the pits

4.6 THE RACE BUILD-UP

- ➤ Noise tests
- ➤ Pre-race checks
- ➤ The assembly area
- ➤ Mental preparation
- ➤ Getting onto the grid
- ➤ Formation and green flag laps
- ➤ Race starts

4.7 RACE DRIVING

- ➤ Smoothness is the key
- ➤ The first corner
- ➤ Being lapped

4.8 WET WEATHER RACING

- ➤ Driving in the rain
- ➤ Aquaplaning
- ➤ Changing conditions
- ➤ Visibility - or lack of it
- ➤ Tyre choice

4.9 PARADE CARS, PACE CARS AND SAFETY CARS

- ➤ Use of parade cars
- ➤ Use of pace cars
- ➤ Use of safety cars
- ➤ The black and yellow flag

4.10 OVERTAKING AND DEFENDING

> ➤ Types of passing move
>
> ➤ The planned move
>
> ➤ The opportunist move
>
> ➤ Defending fairly
>
> ➤ Slipstreaming and dirty air

4.11 LOSING CONTROL

> ➤ Building up to your limit
>
> ➤ The first spin
>
> ➤ Avoiding spinning cars
>
> ➤ Getting onto the grass
>
> ➤ If you have a shunt
>
> ➤ The role of the marshals

4.12 AFTER THE CHEQUERED FLAG

> ➤ The slowing-down lap
>
> ➤ Getting back into the paddock
>
> ➤ The podium
>
> ➤ Checking the gauges
>
> ➤ Parc ferme
>
> ➤ Raised tempers
>
> ➤ De-briefing
>
> ➤ Packing up

4.1 ENTERING YOUR FIRST RACE

Your choice of category will dictate which of the organising clubs you join. Each category with a dedicated championship is owned by one of the clubs that organise motor racing in Britain and to compete in that class you will need to join the relevant club.

See Chapter 7

Typically, racing membership of a major club will cost up to £100 for the year. Once you have joined the appropriate club, you will probably need to register for the championship, once again with the organising club or through the designated championship co-ordinator. Every championship is required to have a co-ordinator and for some of the higher-profile championships, this is almost a full time occupation. For the lesser championships, the co-ordinator is likely to be a volunteer doing the job in their spare time.

The first thing to do is to get hold of a set of the championship regulations from the organising club or championship co-ordinator for the class in which you intend to compete. If you are buying a car for the series, you should have acquired these even before you started looking, as they are the rule book for the championship and contain a lot of vital information.

The next step is to register for the championship. Most classes, though not all, require you to register and in some cases there will be a further registration fee. This should be no more than a modest administration charge and you should be wary of classes where a substantial registration fee is required. This may, in some cases, be a contribution towards the promotion or television coverage of the series, but check what you are getting in return before parting with your cash.

Once you have registered - and you can normally do this at any stage of the year if you are starting mid-season - you will go on the mailing list to receive event regulations. These are the specific regulations for each race meeting and also comprise the entry form which you will need to complete and return to the secretary of the meeting.

Usually, entries for a particular meeting open well in advance of the meeting and close approximately two weeks before the date of the meeting. This allows the organisers to prepare a timetable, allocate paddock space and mail out the final instructions to each competitor. Included with your final instructions (often just known as finals) will be your circuit entry tickets so it is important not to leave them behind. In some higher level categories, teams may be issued with permanent passes at the start of the season.

The entry forms are straightforward and cover the basic information that the organisers need. Amongst other things, you will need to supply details of the car you are driving, your competition licence details and whether you are racing at the circuit for the first time or not. The form must be mailed to the secretary of the meeting in good time to arrive before the closing date, along with the appropriate entry fee. In 2000, entry fees for the three major organising clubs were set at around £140 per car, but clubs like the 750 Motor Club have lower charges. Most organisers accept payment by credit card.

If, for some reason, you miss the closing date, you may still be able to arrange a late entry. But this will be at the discretion of the organisers and may be subject to a late entry surcharge. Also, if you are late entering, you may run the risk of being placed on a reserve list if the entry for your race is over-subscribed.

Each circuit is licensed for a maximum number of starters by the MSA, and only that number of cars may start any race. However, the organisers are allowed to permit up to 20% more cars than that to practice. There are two methods of selecting the cars that will start the race in a situation like this.

Normally, if there is only one class within the race, the fastest cars will fill up the grid to the extent of the permitted number of starters. Any cars outside that number will become reserves in the order in which they qualified. Then, should any of the original qualifiers be unable to start the race, reserves will take their place. Sometimes, the organisers may allow the unsuccessful reserves to race in another event for cars of a similar type later in the day.

Alternatively, in a race where there are two or more classes, entries will be accepted on a first-come, first-served basis until the grid capacity is reached. Subsequent entries, which may still arrive before the closing date, will be placed on the reserve list. If the grid limit plus 20% maximum for qualifying is reached, entries may be rejected, or races divided if the timetable allows.

Sometimes, if a grid for a single-class race is over-subscribed and the timing of the meeting allows, the organisers may arrange a qualification race or even two heats and a final. However, the best way of ensuring a place on the grid is always to get your entry in as early as possible.

In your early meetings, check the event regulations carefully and talk to the secretary of the meeting if necessary to see if there is another race you can enter on the same day. This will give you more track time and, hopefully, two signatures on your racing licence. However, you can only get a maximum of two upgrading signatures per meeting.

4.2 TESTING: WHEN, WHERE AND HOW MUCH?

The level of resource, both time and money, that you have will dictate the amount of testing you do. Some would say that if you can afford to test, do it; if you can't afford to test, then don't. Generally, the amount of testing that goes on increases as you move up the racing ladder. In the leading categories, dedicated test days are arranged at each circuit before the meeting and if you miss the test, you will struggle to be competitive at the race meeting.

Further down the scale, a lot of drivers in the club level categories may only test once before each season, or perhaps not at all. And, it must be said, that good drivers can often be successful without ever testing. However, testing is now an accepted part of the sport, and most circuits are busy at least one day a week with general test sessions.

See Chapter 8.2

Basically, if you are learning about race driving, testing is essential to get you used to handling the car at speed before being thrown into a competitive environment. There is no substitute for time in the car and if you were, for instance, a tennis player, you would expect to train several times a week. At least.

But testing is also a way of spending considerable sums of money and so it should be balanced against available resources. Plus, most testing goes on during week days and if you have a proper job - and without one, you are going to struggle to go racing - getting time off on a regular basis is not going to be easy. Then, of course, you may have to explain to the wife why the family holiday to Spain is off this year because you have used up all your annual holiday going testing!

The choice of where to test is influenced by several factors. Firstly, you will probably want to test at the circuit where you are going to be racing, particularly if you plan to test regularly through the season. Secondly, geographics will most certainly influence where you go. Most people will use their local track for testing whenever possible.

However, when selecting a venue for testing, try and look at the value for money you get. Testing is all about getting the maximum amount of undisturbed track time during the day. Some circuits in the middle of the country will be popular choices, but if sessions are constantly red-flagged by cars spinning into gravel traps, you may not achieve very much.

If you want to get the most from your testing, you may need to travel. Generally, the further away from the middle of the country you go, the quieter the test sessions are likely to be and time and effort spent travelling further afield will often be well-rewarded by quality track time.

Venues like Anglesey, Croft, Pembrey and Snetterton can be a fair trip for many, but it really could be worth the effort.

If you are simply looking for a pre-season shake-down for car and driver, make contact with the club that organises your championship or the relevant co-ordinator, as there may be an exclusive pre-season test day for that particular class. Finally, if you compete in a road-going or near standard car, it is worth checking out some of the various track driving clubs as you may be able to take part in one of their track days.

4.3 THE FIRST RACE DAY

The final instructions will normally arrive in the post early in the week preceding the race meeting. Most officials are convinced that racing drivers never read these, and they are probably right. But you owe it to yourself to study them carefully and make sure you understand any specific instructions relating to the particular circuit, the timetable for the meeting and anything that relates to the race you have entered. A few minutes spent reading and absorbing the finals, could save all sorts of last-minute dramas on race day.

At your first race meeting, and the first time you race at a new circuit, you are required to attend a new driver briefing. The timing of these briefings (there will probably be more than one during the morning of the meeting) will be noted in the final instructions and it is essential that you attend. The briefing will usually be conducted by the Clerk of the Course or one of his deputies and will give you information about any specific rules or aspects of the particular circuit.

The meeting timetable will also denote the times at which you need to sign-on and present your car for scrutineering. At signing-on you will need to produce all your documents, including your racing licence, club membership cards, championship registration documents and medical certificate. All of these items are essential but you still hear stories of drivers making frantic dashes back home to collect something that is missing. If you live some way from the circuit, you run the risk of not competing if you do not have all of the relevant paperwork with you.

THE RACE MEETING

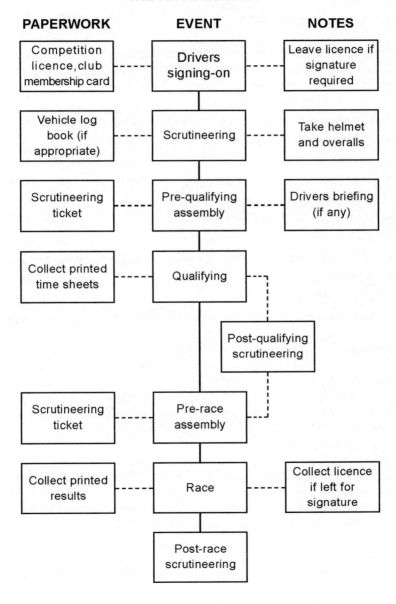

PAPERWORK	EVENT	NOTES
Competition licence, club membership card	Drivers signing-on	Leave licence if signature required
Vehicle log book (if appropriate)	Scrutineering	Take helmet and overalls
Scrutineering ticket	Pre-qualifying assembly	Drivers briefing (if any)
Collect printed time sheets	Qualifying	
	Post-qualifying scrutineering	
Scrutineering ticket	Pre-race assembly	
Collect printed results	Race	Collect licence if left for signature
	Post-race scrutineering	

Typically, there will be a queue at competitors signing-on and so allow some time in your schedule for this. If you are seeking up-grading signatures on your racing licence, remember to leave the licence with the officials at this stage.

Next, you need to get your car to the scrutineering bay so that the official scrutineers can make their safety inspections. The typical things that the scrutineers will be looking at closely include:

- **Wheels and tyres (are there any obvious defects?)**
- **Suspension and steering (is there any play?)**
- **Drivers seat (is it safe and securely anchored?)**
- **Mandatory external cut-out switches (do they work as intended?)**
- **Fuel tank (is it secure?)**
- **Battery (is it fitted securely?)**
- **Fire extinguisher (is the mandatory system fitted securely?)**
- **Brakes (are there any obvious signs of leaking fluid or damaged lines?)**
- **Helmet and overalls (do they meet current regulations?)**

There is much more that the scrutineers may choose to inspect, but the above are the basics. To be honest, if you are going to strap yourself into the car and race it, you should have checked and double-checked these items anyway! It is worth getting into the habit of using check lists or work lists for race meetings, routine items to check before qualifying and then between qualifying and the race. Checking wheel nuts should be very high on the list!

Signing-on and scrutineering can take some time and there is a danger that you will find yourself running out of time before the start of the qualifying session. Best advice is to allow even more time than you think is necessary and get to the circuit in good time.

Many teams prefer to arrive at the circuit the night before a race so that possible delays on the journey are eliminated. Most final instructions will carry a paddock plan showing where competitors in your particular race are expected to park and you should follow this plan at all times. Not only will this benefit the organisers in being able to find you quickly if needed, it may also help you if you need assistance or spares from fellow racers! In the more professional categories, great importance is placed upon paddock layout and the overall image it presents. For these classes, the championship co-ordinator is likely to be on hand when teams arrive to organise parking up so that the paddock has a very professional look. Specific times for arrival and parking up may also be given in the final instructions for the meeting.

If you can, when you are doing your research at race meetings about which class to contest, try and familiarise yourself with the paddock layout and the position of things like the signing-on office and scrutineering bay. This will all save valuable time on race day. If in any doubt, ask. Your fellow racers will usually be happy to point you in the right direction.

You will probably find the time between scrutineering (for which there will usually be a queue) and qualifying tending to evaporate. Therefore, it is sensible to have the car ready for qualifying before going to scrutineering. Things like changing tyres, fuelling up and so on are best done before scrutineering. Then, should you hit a snag at scrutineering and have to fix a last minute problem, you don't have to worry about the routine items. Running out of fuel on the first lap of qualifying would be enormously frustrating for you, and the subject of great mirth for your competitors!

When you have successfully completed scrutineering, keep a tight hold on the ticket that the officials will give you to confirm that your car has passed. As soon as possible, stick it somewhere secure and visible on the car, as it will be checked as you enter the assembly area and you will not be allowed onto the circuit without it.

In a saloon car, this is best put just behind the driver inside the rear window where it is easily seen and checked by the marshals. On a sports-racing car or single-seater, attach it firmly inside the cockpit, ideally positioned so that the driver can point to it easily when stopped for the check. Make sure it is attached securely, ideally with tank tape, and not likely to blow away as soon as you head out onto the circuit.

71

If you do have problems at scrutineering, do not lose your temper with the officials. They are, in some ways, there to protect racing drivers from themselves. If they pick you up on a particular point, it is for your own safety. There is little point trying to dispute their verdicts on safety matters, it is up to you to be prepared and get the problem fixed to their satisfaction.

You are always looking to buy yourself as much time as possible so that when you are called up for qualifying, you have plenty of time in hand and you are well prepared. It is very easy to run out of time to do all the things that need to be done before you and the car are ready to take to the track.

It is useful to display the meeting timetable somewhere prominently around your team (on the side of the tow van, for instance), so that everyone can check at a glance how much time you have. The really professional teams mount a dry-wipe board inside the transporter or awning with all relevant times noted and often have a large clock attached for good measure!

Finally, in the rush and excitement to get the car ready to go onto the track, you must never forget about the safety of anyone working on the car. If the car is jacked up, make sure that proper axle stands are in place. Recently, a driver suffered severe head injuries while he was working under his car when it fell off the jack. Also, take extra care when refuelling or doing any welding on the car. The paddock, and indeed the pits, can be a place of great danger.

4.4 QUALIFYING

As you start qualifying, which will typically be only 15 or 20 minutes long, you should have a plan for the session. The minimum length of the qualifying session is dictated by the circuit length. If the circuit is less than one mile, the session must be at least 10 minutes; for circuits between 1 mile and 2.5 miles, a minimum 15 minutes is specified; for circuits over 2.5 miles, the minimum is 20 minutes.

The most critical requirement is to safely complete three laps, as this is the mandatory minimum to qualify you to race. If you fail to do three laps, you are at the mercy of the Clerk of the Course. Depending upon the timetable for the meeting, he may allow you to do three laps in a later qualifying session. But in such a case, you will then have to start your race from the back of the grid, 10 seconds after everyone else has started.

Generally, your first flying lap is not the most important one of the session. By taking those first three laps fairly steadily you will be able to bring car, driver, tyres and brakes up to working temperature! In the very professional classes, things may well be different as the first flying lap on brand new tyres is all-important. But for most newcomers, this is irrelevant and a steady build up to racing speed is much more sensible.

On the first lap out of the pits take a good look at the circuit conditions, and pay particular attention to the marshals' posts. All of them will be displaying a green flag for the opening lap of the session to remind you of their position. However, even more important to check is whether any of them are displaying the oil or slippery surface flag.

This may be used to identify an oil slick that has been treated with cement dust, or an area where a spinning car in the previous session has thrown grass, mud or water across the track. The same applies, of course, to the green flag lap prior to the race. Be warned also that, while the application of cement to an oil slick will have reduced the chances of sliding on the oil, it can also generate a cloud of dust when cars cross it at high speed. Be ready for a partial loss of visibility if there has been a major oil slick.

In the assembly area, you may see the more experienced drivers rushing to be first in the queue. This is so that they can be first onto the circuit and then, hopefully, have a clear track ahead of them early in the session so that they can push hard for a good qualifying time. Less experienced drivers need not get involved in this 'first race of the day'.

Join the queue of cars somewhere in the middle and, ideally position yourself behind someone who is reasonably quick and not prone to falling off! That way, you may be able to follow them and learn in the early laps. But don't just follow anyone, as you may end up behind someone with even less of a clue than you have!

If you have been to the circuit before and are familiar with it, try and find some clear track during qualifying. Frequently, you will hear drivers complain of traffic during qualifying. The number of cars on the track meant that they had been unable to get a clear lap in which to really push for a time. Racing around in a group during qualifying may be great fun, but it will seldom produce a good lap time.

Frequently, you will see experienced drivers coasting around during a session, looking for a gap in the traffic. If you choose to do this, be very aware of cars coming up behind you quickly and stay well off the racing line. Ruining someone else's hot lap while trying to find space for your own will probably earn you some harsh words in the paddock.

Around 15 minutes after the end of the session, the organisers will publish the complete list of times for the session. Printed copies can be collected from Race Administration (usually the same place as competitors' signing-on) and will show you how you have fared. Typically, the time sheets will show the best lap for each driver and on which lap they set their best time.

The time sheets will be followed by the grid sheet that will give a schematic view of how the cars will line up on the grid. Modern timekeeping systems are incredibly accurate and reliable, but it is possible that you may feel that the timekeepers have not picked up your best lap. In such a case, register your query at Race Administration and ask if the timekeepers can re-check the times.

4.5 PIT SIGNALS

Hopefully, you will have encouraged some friends or family to come along to the meeting and help out. There are many useful jobs they can do, none more so than working your pit board during qualifying. Good quality pit signalling boards are not too expensive and are a good investment.

Once equipped with a stop-watch, your pit crew can give you valuable information on your board. Make sure that your board is easily identified by putting something distinct across the top. A nickname is a useful way of making your board quickly identified from 20 others that may otherwise look the same as you hurtle past the pits. If your loved one calls you

'Fluffy Bunny', it will certainly stand out but don't expect any mercy from your rivals!

Just what information your pit crew display on your board is very much a matter of preference and you will almost certainly fine tune

PIT SIGNALS

it to your own particular choice as you gain experience. As a start-off point, the basics you should have are your latest lap time, the fastest time done by anyone else (in your class if it is a multi-class race) and the amount of time remaining in the session.

Don't forget that your own lap time will be for the previous lap and so the information will always be a lap in arrears. By looking at other pit boards, your crew should be able to get an idea of what is the best time in the session so you have an idea how you are doing.

If you have been to the track before, perhaps for testing, and are now suddenly two seconds a lap slower, seeing the best times from other drives will help you assess whether the track is slower for everyone or if you are losing time. Many circuits will vary from day to day in the lap times that are possible and you will hear talk of fast and slow days. Many factors can have an impact on this.

Ambient temperatures, the amount of rubber and oil on the track and weather conditions can affect the circuit. It is very frustrating to throw your car into a gravel trap trying to match a time you did in testing, only to find that the whole field is going two seconds a lap slower! There is a theory about Donington that the amount of grip available is affected by aviation fuel from aircraft flying into East Midlands airport, which is situated right next to the circuit. Of course, if you are going slower but no-one else is, you have a problem either with the car or the driver which may, or may not, be fixable before the race.

If you are racing on a programme with some higher profile classes like Formula 3, get your crew to take a look around the pit garages as there may well be direct links from the timekeepers to TV monitors. In this case, they will have very exact information which is updated every time a car crosses the start line. Otherwise, there is no substitute for a pair of stop watches and a steady hand. The time remaining is usually shown as, for instance T10, when there are 10 minutes to go.

Also, try and keep to abbreviations that you have agreed with your crew before the session. If the lap times for your class are in the region of 1m 30s, you don't really need to be told about the 1m. A display of 31.2 will be enough for you to know how you are doing. If you have invested in a data logging or 'hot-lap' system of some sort, you will have your lap times displayed in front of you.

See Chapter 5.5

Try and arrange with your pit crew roughly where they will position themselves on the pit wall. Make sure that when you come past the pits for the first time, which will be at reduced speed, they hang the board out even though there is no time to be displayed. This will help you get a fix on where to look on future laps.

The crew need to hold the board out fully for as long as your car is in sight and until it is well past them. Depending on circumstances, you may grab a look at your board at any time during the period in which it is visible. Many wives and girl-friends are willing timers and pit signallers as it gives them a chance to be involved and also occupies their mind while you are rushing round the track.

In the race, you will need different information on your pit board. Most drivers will want to know their position, the number of laps to go and the time gap to either the car ahead or the car behind, or both. However, some more experienced drivers like to see their lap times so that they can tell if they are being consistent.

As you gain experience, you may well develop more than one pit board strategy to suit differing scenarios. Ultimately, it is very much down to personal preference and making sure that you and your crew both understand what is going to happen. Should you be fortunate enough to find yourself in the lead of the race, it is vital to know the gap to the car behind you. Then, if you are pulling away, you can pace yourself accordingly and avoid taking unnecessary risks or pushing the car too hard.

While the pit crew can give you some information, you should also be able to work out much of what is going on for yourself. Knowing your rivals and the colours of their cars can help and, particularly in shorter races, just having a good look around you will tell you much of what you need to know. Some circuits lend themselves to looking across a corner to see who is where, but be careful not to miss your braking point while watching the leaders having a great battle!

If you are likely to be lapped during a race, it is also worth taking a close look at the cars towards the front of the grid. Then, when they come up behind, you will be ready to keep out of their way.

Whilst on the subject of the pits, you must be aware of rules concerning the use of the pits. Just as in Grand Prix racing, there will be a speed limit for the pit lane, but you will not have the luxury of an electronic speed governor like the Formula One cars.

Also, make sure you know which lanes are for working on the car. Typically this is the lane closest to the garages, the other lanes are for cars moving through the pits. If you start to work on the car in one of the other lanes, you will be moved on by the pit marshals. Often, the pit exit will be manned by a marshal who will give you the OK signal, sometimes a green light, when it is safe to join the track. At other circuits, you will accelerate out of the pit lane and merge in with the other cars as though joining a motorway. It is important not to cross the yellow line that extends from the pit exit. Stay within the white line as you accelerate and only start to move across the track after the white line has ended. Whichever, take a good look in your mirrors as you accelerate out of the pits.

Finally, clearly signal your intention to go into the pits by putting your hand up clearly if in an open car. If you are in a saloon with indicators, try and use them as you head for the pits. During testing, find out where the pit entry is before you need it for the first time in anger. Limping around the track for another full lap with a sick motor will not endear you to fellow competitors or race officials.

4.6 THE RACE BUILD-UP

After qualifying, particularly if you have not qualified as well as you had hoped, you may be tempted to tinker with the car and change suspension settings, for instance. While this may well be appropriate for more experienced racers, it is not advised for novices. Changing the car before the race will mean you start the first racing lap with an unknown quantity and thereby take a major risk. The car is best left alone in such circumstances unless you are convinced that it is so bad, that you could not possibly make it any worse!

About 30 minutes before the start of your qualifying session or race your class will be called over the paddock tannoy system to go to the assembly area. Ideally, you should have warmed the engine up before moving up the assembly area as it is often the case that mandatory noise tests will be carried out as you enter the assembly area, either before the qualifying session or before the race.

This will entail revving the car to specified revs and then holding those revs while the noise meter is read. It is not advisable to do this with a cold engine. The current noise limits and methods of testing are covered in the 'Blue Book'. You will then wait while the preceding qualifying session or race is completed. By this stage, you need to have covered everything that needed to be done to the car.

As a matter of routine, you should have checked that there is enough fuel in the car, that tyre pressures are correct and that the wheel nuts are properly torqued up. If you don't take the car to the assembly area yourself, it is worth making sure that your helmet, gloves and balaclava go with the car. A sprint back across the paddock is not the ideal preparation for the race! Allow yourself plenty of time to get strapped in and comfortable in the car before you have to go out onto the track.

Before the race, you will normally be lined up in grid order in the assembly area, with the front of the grid going out first so that the field arrives on the grid in the correct order. This is a good time to take a close look at the cars that will be around you on the grid. Then, when you assemble on the grid, you will know where you are meant to be in relation to the other cars.

If you have any doubt about the procedure for getting onto the grid and then the starting system, make sure you ask an official at this stage. Ideally, particularly if you are racing at a circuit for the first time, go and watch the start of one of the earlier races so that you get a feel for the various signals. It is vital to find out where the starting lights are before you get to the grid. Races have been lost before now when drivers have been gazing around still trying to spot the lights when the race starts. The location will vary from track to track.

Watching another race start will also confirm the countdown procedure as each circuit has its own peculiarities. If it is a busy meeting, and most of them are, do not expect a minute to be the same as 60 seconds. Although the countdown boards will generally show three, two and one minutes to go, the intervals between the boards can be as little as 20 seconds!

However, be warned that start procedures can vary for different types of race and a careful study of the final instructions sent to you by the race organisers will highlight any specific information about your race. Make sure that you know how many laps your race is to be run over so that, should the car develop a fault, you can make a considered decision whether to carry on or not. If you have covered all of this detail beforehand, you should feel slightly more comfortable at what is already a highly stressful part of the race. There is no substitute for being prepared.

In the final minutes before the start of the race, allow yourself a few minutes to think and focus on the start and the race ahead. Most races at national level will have a standing start and it is worth just thinking through the start in terms of what gear you will use and how many revs you need to get the car off the line.

When the green flag is waved to signify the start of the green flag lap (assuming that you are getting one), don't just floor the throttle and rush off. Let the cars ahead of you start to move first and then pull away. Usually, it will take a second or two for the effect of the green flag to work down the grid, particularly if you are towards the back of a full grid.

Driving into the back of the car in front of you as the green flag lap starts will not endear you to anyone. Least of all the driver who gets punted out of the race before the start and the officials of the meeting who have to delay the race to clear up the wheels and fibreglass left on the track as testimony to your eagerness!

Give yourself a bit of space this time around, there is nothing to gain and plenty to lose. As you accelerate away, try and get a feel for the amount of grip that your particular part of the grid has to offer. Cement dust laid on dropped oil, damp patches and even the white lines painted for the grid will have an effect on how much grip you can find.

Practice starts and excessive weaving are officially prohibited during the green flag lap but common practice is to complete something akin to a racing start as you leave the grid. This is an opportunity that some drivers take to try and get heat into the tyres of the driving wheels and also, for more powerful cars on slick racing tyres, to lay some rubber onto the tarmac.

Then, at the end of the green flag lap as you reform on the grid, two black streaks of rubber are ahead of you and the car should be positioned to take full advantage of this. The theory behind this practice is that rubber against rubber is more adhesive than rubber onto clean tarmac!

If you have a problem going into the green flag lap and, for instance, need a push start from the marshals, and are the last car in the field you must keep station at the back of the field and start from the back of the grid. Do not try and drive through the grid to your rightful position, as you will almost certainly be penalised. If, however, you are able to get going before the last car in the pack passes you, it is permitted to re-take your correct grid prosition.

If you start from an incorrect grid position, or are adjudged to have started moving before the green light, you are likely to attract a time penalty. This is commonly referred to as a jump start penalty, but in fact it should be termed a false start penalty as the official judges can penalise a driver for starting from the wrong position as well as for anticipating the start.

Depending upon the judges, you may also be penalised if you move forward before the green light and then stop again. Even if you are stationery when the lights go green, you may still be penalised for a false start. In races of less than 30 miles, the penalty is 10 seconds. If the race distance is more than 30 miles, the penalty is one minute which is added to your time taken for the race. The judges at Castle Combe are particularly noted for their diligence in spotting false starts!

In a race with a rolling start, a penalty may be added for a driver who fails to maintain his correct grid position on the approach to the green light, and thereby gains an advantage over his rivals.

You will often see cars weaving from side to side during the green flag lap to try and build up heat in slick racing tyres. Experts say that such lateral movement does not generate very much extra heat in the tyres, but it will prevent them losing any heat you may have generated earlier in the lap or when leaving the grid. Further, it will help keep the tyres clean.

A race track is covered in rubber debris from previous races and it is important to try and keep your tyres free from this rubbish during the green flag lap. This debris, commonly known as marbles will gather just off the racing line, while the racing line itself will remain much cleaner. If the circuit is particularly dirty, it is probably better to run the green flag lap on the racing line without weaving, rather than risk picking up rubbish on your tyres.

If the circuit has gravel traps on the outside of bends, the marbles could well include pieces of gravel. This is particularly the case if a car has gone off into a gravel trap but been able to keep its momentum going and rejoin the track. In doing so, the car will leave gravel all over the place at that corner. Further, watch out at the next corner as the first time the errant car brakes heavily. It is typical for a shower of gravel to fly out onto the track.

Whilst generating and retaining heat in tyres is very important, it is equally necessary to get brakes up to full working temperature. Customary practice is to drive part of the green flag lap with your left foot on the brakes to generate heat by dragging. If you do this, keep a wary eye on your mirrors to make sure that you don't have someone right on your tail. Similarly, if you do weave from side to side, keep your lateral movement across the track as limited as possible and watch carefully for other cars. Before now, two cars weaving have met in the middle of the track and two drivers have gone for an early bath! As a general rule, never exceed more than half of the track width, or you could be in trouble with the officials.

The process of dragging the brakes up to temperature is particularly important for more powerful cars that are likely to demand brakes that work at a much higher temperature. You need to find out about the brakes on your car and, if necessary, take expert advice from the brake manufacturer about optimum working temperatures. It is, however, possible to overheat the brakes if you generate too much temperature on the warming-up lap but also be warned that some incredibly effective braking systems barely work at all until they reach a suitable temperature.

Of course, some cars will always run short on brakes long before the end of the race. Usually, these will be classic cars from a certain period that may not even have disc brakes all round. If you are racing a classic car, you may need to adopt a different approach altogether to avoid a pedal to the floor crisis later in the race! This may also apply to heavier sports and saloon cars. Equally, ambient temperatures and the demands of the circuit will also have an effect on brake efficiency.

The Grand Prix circuit at Donington is noted as being particularly hard on brakes. The layout of the circuit means that drivers are hard on the brakes three times in quick succession on each lap as they slow down for the Esses, the Melbourne Hairpin and Goddards. With little chance to cool down between each braking zone, many cars run out of brakes before the end of 10 laps on this circuit, even though they have no problems anywhere else. As with every aspect of motor racing, experience is everything!

4.7 RACE DRIVING

Good race driving is all about smoothness. You must strive to make seamless transitions from brake to accelerator and back again, and be as smooth as possible with steering inputs. A racing car is a mass of metal rushing along and its natural tendency is to carry on in the same direction. Making sudden movements on the steering will only serve to unsettle the car.

The components of speed are smoothness, consistency and accuracy. If you master these, you're driving will naturally flow. If you try to force the pace, you will be likely to make more errors.

The best advice for the first corner of the race is to be patient, yet alert for anything that may happen. You probably cannot win the race at the first corner, but you can certainly lose it. In your first few races, the main priority should always be to finish, and heroic dives at the first corner are not recommended. You will gain little experience of racing while sitting on the wall on the outside of the first corner watching the marshals dragging your car out of the gravel trap.

Even 10-lap races are a reasonable length and there is too much at stake to risk banzai first corner moves. Obviously, if an opportunity presents itself and you are decisive and confident, then take it, but measure the risk you may be taking. Most racing accidents happen at the first corner and can be attributed to a combination of cold tyres, cold brakes and, most of all, lukewarm brains!

If you are at the front of the grid with a real chance of winning the race, the first corner can be decisive in the final outcome. If you are further back in the field, self-preservation must be the priority. Try and be aware of the cars around you, for even if you have taken your sensible pills before the race, some of your rivals may not. There is only one thing more frustrating than taking yourself out of the race at the first corner, and that is being taken out by someone else!

Should you lose a place or two at the first corner, you have another 10 laps to try and take them back. Of course, winning is likely to be a distant dream at this stage in your racing career. In your early races, the closest you are likely to get to the race leaders is when they lap you. Do not despair. Legend has it that Damon Hill came close to retiring to the pits and quitting there and then when he made his four-wheeled racing debut.

The safest advice when you are about to be lapped is to keep to your normal line and let the leaders find a way around you. Stories of races being lost by errant backmarkers are legion and if a race leader is taken out by a backmarker, the slower car will automatically be considered the culprit, whatever the truth of the situation.

Often, the leader will have seen you ahead for a lap or more before he catches you up. That won't always happen, but is quite common. In that situation, he will have seen your line through various corners and will have planned a passing move accordingly. Even if you haven't had anyone behind you in the early part of the race, you should always check your mirrors regularly as the leader could come upon you very suddenly.

And, of course, a faster car may be recovering after a spin or a pit stop. You must stay vigilant at all times and, if you are near the back of the grid, it is worth doing some quick calculations before the race. Take the difference between the pole position time and your best lap. Then multiply that by the number of laps in the race. If the resulting time is more than the pole position lap time, there is every chance that you will be lapped. This calculation will also give you a fair estimate of on which laps you should expect the leaders to arrive behind you.

Most leading drivers will prefer the backmarker to stay on his line and maintain the same pace. If the backmarker, with the best of intentions, suddenly lifts off, the leader may be taken by surprise, having planned his move taking into account the relative speed differentials. If you do move out of the leaders way, make a bold signal about which way you are going and be very careful that the leader is on his own.

Many times, an obliging backmarker has pulled out of the leader's way only to find himself in the path of the other car that was fighting for the lead. Having the race leaders go either side of you can be pretty scary, but that is preferable to moving out of the way of the leader and putting the second-placed car off the road because you didn't know he was there.

4.8 WET WEATHER RACING

There is one certainty about the British climate. Between March and October it will rain and you will be very lucky to go through a season of racing without having at least one wet race. Most drivers either love or loathe wet-weather racing. Generally, it is seen as a great leveller, giving talented drivers the chance to shine in conditions that may not suit the drivers with the most powerful cars. In extremely wet conditions, the smaller, less-powerful cars can have a distinct advantage as excessive power can simply be an embarrassment on a very wet track.

WET WEATHER RACING

There is no substitute for experience when it comes to racing in the rain. Invariably, visibility will be poor as plumes of spray are sent up from the cars and in the early laps of the race, drivers in the mid-field can be driving almost blind as they try and peer into a wall of spray kicked up by the leading cars. This can be very nasty, and a cautious approach is demanded, even if you lose time on the leading cars as a result.

Just as you would on a slippery road, wet race tracks require a delicate approach using less revs than usual and allowing greater margins for error. Local knowledge of the circuit can be of great importance when the weather gets really bad as puddles can form or water can run across the track in rivers as it drains from the run-off areas. Only experience can warn you about the likelihood of this, and when you race on a track for the first time in the wet, you must be extra-vigilant.

If conditions are so bad that puddles may be forming, try and chat to a more experienced racer while you are in the assembly area as they may well be able to tell you about notorious sections of the track. Aquaplaning off the track is a scary experience and, particularly in low-slung sportscars and single seaters, drivers can be easily caught out.

Such are the vagaries of our weather that, on some days, you may find one section of the track dry and the next one wet. If you are racing on slicks, you could face some major problems. In this type of situation, the race organisers may stop the race on grounds of safety and allow teams to change to wet weather tyres.

Don't forget that if the track has recently dried out from a rain storm, the grass run-off areas are likely to still be very wet and, therefore, incredibly slippery. Slick tyres don't have much grip on wet tarmac; on wet grass they have no grip whatsoever. The best advice for racing safely in the rain is to extend braking distances, reduce maximum revs and try taking corners in the next gear up.

You should also pay attention to driver comfort and visibility in such conditions. In an open car you are going to get wet and nothing will prevent it. But you need to make sure your visor stays as clear as possible, both on the inside and outside. Various treatments are available to either disperse water on the outside or prevent misting on the inside.

You may not have this problem in a closed car, but keeping the screen clear is just as important. Efficient windscreen wipers and some form of ventilation are essential, though these seem to be requirements frequently ignored by racers until they are needed, and then it's too late!

On a wet day, make sure you dry off the soles of your racing boots as you get into the car as the last thing you need is your foot slipping off the brake pedal as you dive into the first corner. If you race wearing spectacles, try and spend a few minutes outside before getting into the car so that your glasses have a chance to adapt to the ambient temperature. If you wear glasses and have ever walked into a warm pub on a cold night, you will know what a problem this can be. It is bad enough being unable to find your way to the bar, but even more embarrassing if you can't find your way to the correct grid position!

On a day of changing weather, the worst conditions for many drivers, you will see teams in the assembly area casting anxious glances at the sky. Suddenly, you have a crowd of weather forecasters all trying to decide what the weather is going to do for the next 30 minutes. It is a situation that most drivers hate, as critical decisions have to be made and many races have been won, and lost, on these decisions.

For classes running one specification of treaded tyre it is not so bad, but for classes that have the choice of running slicks, it can be an awful dilemma. Each situation is different, and more experienced drivers will often gamble on slicks if there appears to be a chance of the track drying. However, newcomers would be better advised taking the safe option of staying on wet tyres if the track was less than dry.

Often, frantic activity precedes the race as teams make their choices and it can sometimes be a cat-and-mouse affair as rivals wait to see what each other is doing before making a final choice. And, of course, it is not just tyres that may need to be changed at the last minute, as suspension settings like anti-roll bars are often adjusted to suit the conditions.

An important factor at this stage, is to check with the organisers if they are declaring the race wet. This is a decision that the Clerk of the Course has to make and communicate to the drivers and it can have a big effect on the race. Basically, if the CoC declares a wet race, he has no requirement to stop the race should the rain return or become heavier, unless further problems arise. Any driver opting for slicks in such a situation is on his own and must make his own decision about continuing if conditions worsen.

However, if the race starts on a dry track, the CoC may consider stopping the race if it rains to allow drivers the chance to change tyres. Obviously, this is particularly likely if the cars race on slick tyres. If you have qualified in the dry but the track is wet for racing, you will be allowed two warming-up laps to check out the conditions. A chequered flag will normally be shown as you pass the startline for the first time, warning you that there is another lap to go before you form up on the grid.

Finally, if a driver is caught on treaded tyres on a dry or drying track, he will find the tyres quickly over-heating. A set of wet tyres can be reduced to rubbish in the course of 10 laps on a drying track. In such circumstances, you will often see drivers altering their racing line on the straight to deliberately drive through any remaining wet patches away from the racing line. This is to try and cool the tyres down a little and make them last until the end of the race.

Should you find yourself running wet tyres on a nearly dry track, you really should consider the value of finishing the race against the cost of a new set of wets. They will not last long, and if most of your rivals are on slicks, you are going to plummet down the order anyway!

4.9 PARADE CARS, PACE CARS AND SAFETY CARS

There are three different types of official car that you may come across on the circuit. All have specific uses. First is the parade car, which is sometimes used to control the field as it leaves the assembly areas and makes its way to the grid. The location of the assembly area in relation to the grid varies from track to track. At circuits like Snetterton and Castle Combe, cars can be gridded directly from the assembly area. At others, like Oulton Park and Mallory, cars will normally complete almost a full lap before forming up on the grid.

A parade car will probably be used while cars from the previous race are towed in or removed, or while repairs are made to tyre walls. In this situation, marshals may be working trackside and the driver of the parade car will control the speed of field appropriately.

A parade car may also be used to take the cars around on a green flag lap prior to a standing start, though this is far less common. The norm is for cars to be released on a green flag lap with the pole position car responsible for setting the pace.

A pace car will only be used in conjunction with a rolling start. This type of start is less common in national racing and tends to be used for longer-distance races. However, it is possible that club racers will encounter a rolling start. It is important, during such a start, to hold grid position and only start racing when the lights are switched to green. Being in the right gear at the right time is the key to rolling starts.

A safety car is used to control or neutralise a race. This situation will probably develop as a result of an accident that needs to be cleared by the marshals before racing can resume safely. In a safety car period, the car (with lights flashing) will join the track and endeavour to take position immediately ahead of the race leader. All marshals posts will display a board marked 'SC' and will show a waved yellow flag when the safety car and the following train of cars is in that sector. This will be reverted to a stationary yellow flag when the safety car and following cars move into the next sector.

Should you be confronted with such a situation, and you probably will during a season of racing, it is important to maintain concentration during the laps that you are running round at very reduced speed behind the safety car. Be wary of not getting too close to the car ahead of you as the queue of cars has a tendency to concertina at various points around the lap.

There have been accidents in the crocodile of cars behind the pace car due to inattention. The fact that you were waving to your sponsors in their hospitality suite as you ran into the back of the car ahead of you will take some explaining to an unimpressed Clerk of the Course! Overtaking is forbidden when behind the safety car, unless you are specifically directed to pass by the observer in the safety car.

When the incident is cleared, the flashing lights on the safety car are turned off and the safety car will peel off into the pits at the end of that lap. When the green flag is waved at the startline, racing can resume. Laps run behind the safety car may or may not be counted as racing laps. Currently, this varies between different organisers.

The black and yellow quartered flag is used increasingly to perform a similar function to the safety car. The flag can be deployed at all marshals' posts as a way of neutralising the race. When this flag appears, it is the responsibility of the race leader to act as a safety car and lead the pack around at approximately 50mph.

All the cars in the race should form up behind the leader and follow around in one convoy. Overtaking is again prohibited. The marshals are then able to work in safety, knowing that all the cars are in one particular section of the track. This flag is often used when cars need to be removed from gravel traps by snatch vehicles, and is a very efficient alternative to red flags and re-started races. When the incident is clear, the green flag at the start line signals that racing can resume. In most classes, all laps run under the black and yellow flag count as racing laps.

The final instructions for the meeting will cover exactly what system is to be used for controlling a race in this type of situation. The finals will also detail whether laps run under control will count as race laps or not. Once again, it is essential that you understand exactly what will happen and what you need to do when confronted with such a situation. Clerks of the

Course will show little mercy in dealing with drivers who obviously have not taken the time to read their finals!

4.10 OVERTAKING AND DEFENDING

The golden rule for overtaking is to be decisive. If you hesitate part-way through an overtaking manoeuvre, either the move will not work or you take the risk of colliding with the car you are trying to pass. If you are decisive, you should be able to carry out the move.

OVERTAKING AND DEFENDING

There are really two different types of overtaking manoeuvre between cars and drivers of similar performance. The planned variety where you build up to it, possibly over a number of laps, and the opportunist move where an error from the driver in front provides you with the opportunity of overtaking.

The planned move can be executed in several different points around the lap. The obvious places are under braking for a corner or under acceleration out of a corner. Out-braking a rival into the corner probably means that you have been chasing them down the preceding straight. Realistically, you will have to at least match the speed of the other car down the straight and, in itself, that speed may be the product of a faster exit from the corner leading onto the straight.

Obviously, in a race situation where the cars are of very different specification, it is possible to lose ground to a rival on the straight, then pull back all the lost ground under braking and still execute a successful passing move. But, in evenly-matched cars this will simply not be possible.

In mixed class races, braking distances will vary tremendously and knowledge of your rival's capabilities is very important. However, if you are able to sail past into the corner under braking, the chances are that the other car will then blast you into the weeds under acceleration out the corner. This could well be frustrating, but the crowds love a good cat and mouse contest!

If you plan to outbrake your rival into a corner, be wary of them trying to protect their line. This is the start of one of the most common accidents found in racing, as the leading driver tries to defend the corner when his rival is partly alongside. Frequently the cars will touch and both could spin out of the race.

Ideally, you need to catch your rival by surprise when making such a move so that by the time they realise what is happening, you are already up alongside them and leaving no chance for them to turn into the corner across the front of your car. If you can, keep your planned move under wraps until the lap you mean to carry it through.

However, there can be a problem with this. Your move on the inside for the corner is likely to take you into an area of the track you have not previously used. At the very least, on the lap before you mount your bid, take a good look at the track surface for the tighter entry line to the corner. This should alert you to any debris on the track or even any lingering damp patches that could catch you out.

If you have followed your rival for several laps, you should have been able to work out where you have an advantage, as most drivers are reasonably consistent. In this situation, try and not make it obvious where your advantage lies. If you start showing an advantage in certain corners, you are encouraging your rival to defend in the very place where you want to attack. It all comes down to planning ahead.

Many classic outbraking moves start at least one corner before the one where the move is planned. A well-known move is at Paddock Hill Bend and Druids at Brands Hatch. However, a successful pass into Druids may well have started back at Clearways. If you make a faster exit at Clearways, you should be able to be on the attack towards Paddock. The classic move is to feint to the inside going into Paddock so as to force your rival to defend the inside line.

At the last moment, the attacker switches back to the outside and normal racing line into Paddock, leaving the leader committed to a tighter line. This will inevitably force the leading car wide on the exit and the attacker should be able to take a quicker run through Paddock having regained the proper racing line. That greater exit speed may well be enough to pull the attacker's car alongside at the foot of the hill and claim the inside line for Druids.

It all sounds very easy, of course, and watching an expert execute such a move it can seem very simple. But it is far from easy and can take a lot of mastering. When you do it for the first time, you will be elated!

Overtaking in the middle of a corner is less common, but can be equally as effective. Generally it would be done on the outside line but does entail some risk and, ideally, should only be tried on a driver in whom you have a degree of trust! If you find that the car in front is consistently moving to the inside under braking to protect the line into the corner, then you could take a more traditional racing line into the corner and carry greater entry speed.

That extra momentum could allow you to go round the outside in the first half of the corner. Then, as you reach the apex of the corner, you are still going past the other car and have the momentum to carry you out of the corner. If you are fully alongside by the time the cars reach the apex of the corner, your presence will force the rival to maintain a tight line through the corner with a consequent loss of speed.

By taking the outside line into the second half of the corner, you now have the optimum exit line and can make full use of the width of the track as you exit the corner. But beware, some less honest drivers may be tempted to squeeze you out wide on the exit of the corner and you could find yourself up the kerbs and onto the grass! However, most drivers at club level will allow you enough room in a situation like this.

Ideally you must get to know the people you are racing with, and then you will be able to make a judgement about trying such a move. In fact, this knowledge will have a significant bearing on the type of overtaking move you use in the race.

When you make an opportunist move, you may, of course, have already been planning a move when suddenly a chance presents itself and then it is a question of how decisively you act upon that opening. This situation can arise in many different ways. If you are chasing the car in front, they may be temporarily held up by a backmarker. This could put them off line or cause them to be slow on the exit of a corner; or they have gone off-line going into a corner; or they have missed a gear on the exit of a corner.

On the first lap of a race, particularly in classes using slick racing tyres, people often make mistakes when their tyres are still cold and not up to optimum working temperature. This could result in a car understeering into a corner and, quite possibly, the same will happen at the next corner while the driver is still trying to generate heat in the front tyres.

If you are alert, you can see all this going on in front of you and be ready to capitalise on the opportunity presented. Once you have spotted your opportunity, you need to position your car in the optimum place on the circuit to ensure a successful pass and counter any prospect of your rival rechallenging. Contrary to what is sometimes displayed at surprisingly high levels of the sport, this does not mean trying to squeeze your rival off the track. There is absolutely no excuse for making contact with another car when overtaking.

Having been given an opportunity, it is important not to gift it straight back. Consider that just about every driver in a race will make at least one mistake, and probably many more. Even the very best drivers make mistakes, so why should less-experienced drivers expect to do otherwise?

Typically, drivers will make one or two mistakes in the first half of a race and then as the race progresses they will start making regular mistakes, as they become more tired and find it harder to maintain concentration. You may find that if you are patient and can keep lapping consistently, you can win races purely by not making mistakes, rather than by pulling off dramatic and daring passing moves.

Putting pressure on the car in front is a widely-use tactic and can encourage the driver ahead to make the mistake that will present the overtaking opportunity. If you are able to at least match the speed of your rival, there is every chance that, if you were able to get ahead, you could pull away. So, if you are doing the chasing it can be worth positioning your car at different points on the circuit to make it look as though you are working out where to overtake.

The move of taking a look into corners can have benefit. What you are trying to do is distract your rival by getting them to look in their mirrors to see where you are. While doing this, they might miss their braking point by a few yards and are generally more prone to making mistakes. It can even be worth positioning your car on a straight so that your rival cannot see you in his mirrors.

They will then be trying to work out where you have gone and it could be that you are already alongside them. Or, importantly, they start to think that you could be! Particularly in sports-racing type cars, rear-vision is severely restricted and racing cars will tend to have an even bigger blind spot than road cars.

When your rival gets to the next corner, they may not be entirely sure just where you are. If this happens, you need to be ready to take full advantage of any gap left by a moment's hesitation. In carrying out such a move, you will have done nothing illegal. You have not deliberately weaved about and neither have you made any contact with the other car. It is simply a racing tactic that can bring profit.

A useful tip is to study the experts. Grands Prix are not currently noted for overtaking, but pay particular attention to how Formula One drivers set about this very difficult task. It can take many laps of patient planning before the move is pulled off. Try to understand exactly what happened during the overtaking move.

Better still, Indy Car racing does generate overtaking and watching some of the star names work their way through traffic, both on ovals and road courses, can be very enlightening. Watch how an overtaking move is built up over the course of several laps. Their talents are there for everyone to watch, so why not take advantage and learn from the best in the world.

Of course, there will probably be just as many cases where you are the one under pressure from a rival and will need to defend your place without resorting to the type of tactics that will earn you an interview with the Clerk of the Course.

The golden rule, sadly ignored by many who should know better, is not to weave about down the straight. The rules are quite clear about this and the MSA Year Book notes that manoeuvres liable to hinder other drivers such as premature direction changes on the straight, crowding of cars to one side of the track and any other abnormal change of direction will be subject to penalty. Equally, any driver consistently hindering or discouraging the passing attempts of another driver is liable to penalty.

It is a sad fact, however, that far too much weaving goes on, even at amateur levels of racing. If someone has clearly got a quicker car than you or is simply driving faster, there is no justification for weaving about on the straight to try and block them. Consider that the day will probably come when you are the one being blocked and, doubtless, you will be highly unimpressed by a driver dodging around in front of you.

If you are in front, it is legitimate to take the line of your choice down the straight. However, once you have chosen your line, you should keep to it. If someone is pressing you, it is important to try and sort out where your weaknesses are. If they have a considerable advantage in straightline speed, you are in trouble! In all probability, they will get past you somewhere, no matter how you approach the corners.

Where a series of corners leads onto a straight, you need to concentrate on getting the most out of your equipment through those corners so that you can maximise any advantage you have as you come onto the straight. Generally, if someone is close behind, you should try to go into the preceding corner slower than you would normally, so that you can concentrate on maximising exit speed.

Should you go barrelling into the corner and, as inevitably will happen, start sliding around, anyone sensible behind you will then accelerate through the corner and easily drive past you on the straight. By slowing your car down carefully into the corner, you will be able to carry exit speed onto the straight. The key is to be hard on the power as early as possible in the corner, whilst not scrubbing speed off on the exit.

Slipstreaming is an art that does have a place in certain classes. The principle is that you use the hole in the air created by the car ahead of you to gain an advantage in a straightline. By having less wind resistance, your car may be able to gain a higher straightline speed than normal and be in a position to pull out and pass your rival towards the end of the straight.

This is fine in some classes, notably those where aerodynamic aids are not permitted. However, in many single seater classes with advanced aerodynamics, slipstreaming will tend not to work. Getting close enough to a rival through a corner to gain a tow on the straight, will leave the attacker running in turbulent air created by the car ahead. This is known as dirty air.

When running in dirty air, the following car will find its aerodynamic balance severely disrupted and the result will be a loss of downforce through the corner! This leads to a loss of corner exit speed and no chance to attack. It is a common problem in modern single seater racing and can make it immensely difficult to overtake a rival in a car of similar performance.

However, slipstreaming still has a place, notably at the faster tracks, in classes like Formula Ford where a lack of wings makes the cars more suitable for the art. Further, the increased speed gained from a good tow can make a big difference to qualifying times in a class like this. During qualifying, it is common to see drivers playing cat and mouse games as they try to receive a tow whilst not giving one away to a rival. Sometimes team-mates will work together to help each other at times like this.

4.11 LOSING CONTROL

LOSING CONTROL

It is a sure fact that, at some stage during your racing, you are going to lose control of the car. How, when and why will vary, but virtually every incident is the result of either driver error or mechanical failure. The result of losing control can range from a mildly amusing moment to a bone-jarring, wallet-rending shunt.

The best way of avoiding too many driver errors is to use test sessions and your early race meetings to build up to your limits gradually, rather than exceeding them and then working back. Of course, many people who start racing want to follow the 'maximum attack' approach, treating every session in the car as the final round of the world championship.

In the excitement of the moment, it is all to easy to forget that the purpose of the test session was to bed in new brake pads and not break the lap record on the second lap out of the pits. Self-control is something that some of us only have in a modest amount, but a lack of it could cost you dear in your early career.

The first time you lose control of the car, and you surely will, it is likely that a fairly harmless spin will be the result. However, even when you finally admit defeat and stop fighting to regain control, you still have work to do. Damage limitation is required urgently. The key things to do are brake and de-clutch. When nearing the end of the spin, if you are still on the tarmac, try and keep your foot on the brake and not let the car roll gently, particularly if there is a natural camber on the track.

Countless times, cars that have spun then roll slowly into the path of another car because the spinning driver didn't keep his foot on the brake. Following cars will naturally aim to avoid a near-stationery car and if it moves another foot or two, there can be disastrous consequences.

However, there is another school of thought for when a car starts to spin in front of you. At this stage of the incident, the best advice from some experienced racers is to aim for where the car is at the time it starts to spin, as typically the spinning car will go either to the left or the right. However, there is no hard evidence to support this, just paddock talk amongst drivers that have been in that situation!

Should you spin and come to a stop in a position where your visibility is obscured, don't just try to rejoin if you cannot see the traffic coming towards you. Look for signals from a marshal for when it is clear to rejoin. If you force other drivers to take avoiding action as you rejoin, quite probably the Clerk of the Course will want to have a chat about it.

If you spin several times during a qualifying session or race, you may also be up before the CoC. It is quite likely that he will refrain from signing your race licence for up-grading from that race. Every spin or incident is reported by the observers positioned around the circuit, so you will be found out. If you do spin more than once, you also need to sit down afterwards and make sure you understand why.

If you are forced off the track by another competitor, or find yourself running wide onto the grass due to an error of your own, you need to do several things to avoid losing control. Don't brake, ease back on the throttle, hold the steering wheel with a very light grip and gently nudge your car back onto the tarmac, trying to watch where other cars are at the same time.

Arriving backwards on the tarmac while scattering fresh grass cuttings across the track like an out of control lawn-mower will not endear you to your fellow competitors!

At some stage you are probably going to park your pride and joy against the tyre wall. There isn't really any good advice in such a situation, but it is sensible not to brace yourself too hard with your feet and hands as the impact could easily break a wrist that was braced against the steering wheel.

If you are completely unhurt and free to move, get out of the car calmly and head for safety as quickly as possible, but before you leave your damaged car, try and check to see that no other cars are heading for you. If you fell off due to oil or a sudden rain shower, the chances are that other drivers may make similar mistakes. Ideally, turn off the electrics before you leave the car as this will save one of the marshals having to go and do this. A stricken car with live electrics presents a greater fire risk.

If you have any doubts about possible injury or are trapped in the car, do not panic. Expert assistance will be on hand in seconds and it is at times like this that you will fully appreciate the efforts of the marshals. They will take control of the situation and summon all the necessary back-up to ensure your safe removal from the car. Put yourself completely in their hands as this is what they are trained for.

The chance of you needing such assistance is pretty rare, but should things go badly wrong, you will be in safe hands. If you are injured or trapped in the car, you will not be moved until expert medical support is on hand. If there is a risk of fire, the marshals on the scene will be on the alert and ready to deal with any small fire that may start. If there is any concern of neck or back injury, you will be stabilised before being moved. It may seem dramatic, but it is standard procedure.

Even if you have vacated the car un-aided, any driver who has had an incident involving contact with the barriers or another car must be seen by the medical officers and you will be asked to report to the medical centre if not taken there by ambulance. Once again, this is for your own safety.

Finally, it is possible that your car will catch fire during a qualifying session or race. An oil leak may be spraying onto a hot exhaust, for instance. If you become aware of this, don't just park the car anywhere you can. Try and spot the nearest group of marshals and park close to them. By saving them having to run 100 yards with heavy fire extinguishers, you could save considerable damage to your car.

Obviously, your own on-board extinguisher system may need to be activated.

4.12 AFTER THE CHEQUERED FLAG

Spinning off on the slowing down lap is a sure-fire way of earning the laughter of spectators, marshals and fellow racers. The important thing is to maintain concentration even after you have passed the chequered flag. Be aware of other cars backing off sharply and avoid doing this yourself. In the drama of the final corner, you may have seen the chequered flag, but the rival who is tucked in behind you may not have seen the flag.

If the first they know of the end of the race is when their car makes sharp contact with the back of yours, it could spoil the day for both of you. So wind the power off steadily and keep a careful watch both ahead and behind for drivers who may not have spotted the flag. If you have brakes lights on your car, brake gradually so that the lights come on as warning to anyone behind you.

As you tour round on the slowing down lap, keep alert as there may be cars about that have been involved in last lap incidents and the marshals will not be impressed if you arrive at racing speed while they are starting to clear up.

Remember to keep your crash helmet on and seat belts tight until you are stationery back in the paddock, and don't overtake on the slowing down lap. This is even more important if you are lucky enough to have won the race. Once over the finish line, never overtake any other cars that are obviously still racing. Not only will you ruin their chances of, perhaps, battling for a class victory, you may even cause them to be classified as non-finishers as they could be waved off the track without taking the chequered flag.

Having slowed down progressively, you will be directed off the track by the marshals. At some circuits, this may be other than into the pit road and you will need to have studied the final instructions or paid attention at the drivers' briefing to find out if you are to return to the paddock by some other route. This regularly happens at several circuits as a means of saving time, so stay alert and don't get caught out.

AFTER THE CHEQUERED FLAG

If you have finished in the top three or are a class winner, you will probably be directed towards the podium, where you will receive the spoils of victory and may get the chance of being interviewed by the commentator. Whether you behave like a Grand Prix driver and waste good champagne by spraying it around, or keep it to share later with your hard-working pit crew is up to you.

However, it is worth remembering that if you are interviewed, the crowd will want to hear from someone who is excited about the race. If you have had a problem with another driver during the race, the podium is not the place to start making accusations. This will only reflect badly on the class of racing, the championship sponsor (if there is one) and any sponsors you may have.

On the slowing down lap, take a look at your instrumentation to see what sort of temperatures, oil pressure and so on your car is showing. They will typically be at their maximum after the rigours of the race and will give you useful data about your car. Try and remember the key values and make a note of them after the race. You may, of course, find that the water temperature is still on the low side against optimum readings and this may lead you to blank off some of the radiator for future races run in similar ambient temperatures.

As soon as you are back in the paddock after the race, try to arrange for your pit crew to take tyre temperatures. Adding this to your file of data will help you build experience about just what your car is doing during the race and is particularly appropriate for classes using slick racing tyres.

As you return to the paddock, watch out for officials holding signs saying 'go to scrutineering.' At higher profile meetings, the whole field will be directed to parc ferme, in other races only selected cars will be directed to post-race scrutineering. Parc ferme is a controlled area where cars are held by officials immediately following the race. Although eligibility checks may only be carried out on selected cars, all cars are held during this process. Pit crews are not admitted to parc ferme and on no account should any work be done on the cars until cleared for release by one of the officials.

At this stage, drivers will still be pumped up with adrenalin after the race and tempers can easily flare if a driver feels that he has been wronged by another. It is absolutely essential, should you feel that another driver has committed a breach of the rules against you, that you do not seek confrontation after the race. Equally, be cautious of being wound-up by the opinions of your pit crew. They are emotionally involved with your racing and may not have seen the full incident.

If you feel unable to discuss the matter rationally, do not approach the other driver. There is always a danger that, in such highly-charged circumstances, a discussion will lead to physical confrontation. If this happens, the drivers involved face the very real prospect of a disciplinary hearing at the MSA and the potential loss of their racing licence. Drivers mounting a physical assault on a rival have been banned from racing for as long as five years.

Your prime course of action is to seek out of the Clerk of the Course and, if necessary, lodge a protest against your rival. However, this should always be seen as a last resort and should be discouraged whenever possible, particularly at club level. In the heat of the moment, your emotions will be running high and it is a good idea to discuss the incident with an independent third-party first of all. The championship co-ordinator, if present at the meeting, is an ideal person to start with.

Remember that there are almost certainly two sides to the incident and if it can be resolved with a hand-shake over a beer in the clubhouse, everyone will go away feeling better about the day. Driver disputes that run from one meeting to the next are not healthy and, after all, this is supposed to be a sport. It may be that a sensible opportunity develops at the next meeting for a calm chat about the incident and it is good to bury the hatchet before taking to the circuit again.

After the race, you will almost certainly want to share the experience with your crew and fellow racers. Tales of heroic moments and ones that got away will abound, and that is all part of the fun of the sport. But it is worth taking a few minutes to note down anything important about the car's performance for future reference. A quick de-brief with your crew may highlight information and data that will be useful when you next race at that particular circuit.

In the professional classes, a driver will often spend an hour or more locked in the motorhome with his engineer going through a lengthy de-brief and pouring over data. This is not very relevant for the amateur categories, but it is good to sit quietly after the race and make some notes while the race is fresh in your mind. Ask your pit crew about the race; where were the leaders changing gear past the pits? Things like this will be useful information and will help you develop your own driving.

Keep a log with all your data. Testing times, qualifying times, race times - all with a note of weather conditions. Include in the log the number of laps completed and relevant temperatures at the end of the session. This log should also be used to record changes made during test sessions and the results of any changes.

Once the car is safely loaded up and all the equipment packed away, don't forget to collect your licence from race administration and pick up a copy of the final results. Along with the qualifying times, it is useful to file these safely as, not only do they record your result, but they also carry useful information about lap times for the whole field during that particular meeting.

CHAPTER 5
GETTING THE BEST FROM YOUR CAR

IN THIS CHAPTER

5.1 SUSPENSION
- Understeer and oversteer
- Springs and dampers
- Bump and rebound
- Anti-roll bars
- Ride heights
- Corner weights
- Camber and castor
- Toe-in and toe-out

5.2 TYRES
- Control tyres
- Racing on road tyres
- Slick and wet tyres
- Tyre temperatures
- Tyre pressures

5.3 AERODYNAMICS
- Wings and downforce
- Straightline speed
- Gurney flaps
- Front wings and splitters

5.4 GEARBOXES AND RATIOS

> ➤ Standard gearboxes
> ➤ Competition gearboxes
> ➤ Changing ratios
> ➤ Sequential and semi-automatic gearboxes
> ➤ Heel and toe
> ➤ Short-shifting and power-shifting

5.5 DATA-LOGGING

> ➤ What data do you need?
> ➤ Dash displays
> ➤ Choosing a system
> ➤ Lap timers

5.1 Suspension

The subject of race car suspension can fill a complete book and several very good works have been written that cover the subject in great detail. They are recommended reading for anyone who wishes to fully explore the subject, particularly if you are involved with a more high-tech class of racing. In this chapter we aim to cover the basics and explain the terms most commonly used.

Before going any further into suspension terminology, it is vital to understand two basic terms. Most of what happens on a race track when a car starts to slide will be either understeer or oversteer. When you turn into a corner and the front of the car tries to slide straight on, you have understeer. When the back end of the car loses adhesion and tries to overtake the front, you have oversteer.

These two characteristics have been described in simple terms; understeer is when the front of the car hits the bank first; oversteer is when the back of the car hits the bank first! You do not want much of either, but a little understeer or oversteer is inherent in most cars. Which you prefer is very much down to personal choice and most drivers have a strong preference for one or the other.

The first things you come across when looking at suspension are the springs. On a lot of racing cars the springs are adjustable in terms of the rating of the springs you can use. The higher the rating of the spring, the stiffer it will be and so allow less roll on the car as it corners. The softer the spring, the more the car will tend to roll around and soak up the bumps on the track surface more easily.

Typically, if time and conditions allow, teams will run softer springs for wet-weather racing, but the British climate does not always allow people the luxury of being able to make a choice. When you first buy your racing car, it is worth having the springs tested to make sure they are correctly marked and working properly. If they have been on the car for several seasons, they could have gone soft.

The shock absorbers (or dampers) are there to control the rate at which the spring compresses. A lot of cars do not have adjustable dampers and so you have to work with what you get. All you can do in this case is check that the dampers are working properly by taking them to the manufacturer or a local specialist to have them checked and serviced. Though damper technology can become expensive, it can also make a very big difference to the performance of the car.

In classes of racing where there is free choice of damper, competition is fierce between rival manufacturers. However, in many classes, controls are imposed on the range of dampers that can be used in order to keep costs in check.

With adjustable dampers, the first adjustment is known as bump. This controls the rate at which the spring compresses under load. When the car hits a bump or starts to lean into a corner, the spring will compress and the damper controls the speed at which the spring compresses. Some more sophisticated dampers also have adjustable re-bound. That is the rate at which the spring recovers from compression and returns to its standard position. Re-bound is the counter to bump.

The settings to be used for bump and re-bound are really down to driver taste in relation to the particular circuit and the car. There is not really a right or wrong setting and this will be one of the things to be experimented with during testing. One of the specialist books on the subject will offer much more detail for those that need it.

However, the importance of these adjustments should not be under-estimated. Drivers have found, sometimes to their cost, that even modest adjustments can have a profound effect on the handling characteristics of the car.

The next item to be considered is the anti-roll bar. Once again, not all cars are fitted with anti-roll bars. This does exactly what it says, it counters roll on the car as it corners. Typically, a racing car will have an anti-roll bar at the front and one at the back. Quite often, particularly on single-seaters, they will be adjustable.

If the roll bars are adjustable, it is worth experimenting with them during testing. Also, check that the bars are working properly with the correct amount of free play and are not seized up. The roll bar must be able to move to actually work, it is not supposed to be solid. Information about roll bar settings should be sought from more experienced competitors. In wet conditions, a lot of drivers disconnect roll bars completely, while for the dry they will run a relatively stiff setting. You will probably hear talk of softening the car up for the rain, and roll bar adjustment is an important part of this process.

When you are building experience during testing, it can be worth going to extremes on roll bar settings. For instance, go to full stiff on the front of the car and leave the rear bar at a medium setting and do a couple of laps. Then, return to the pits and disconnect the front bar completely and try a few more laps.

You should notice an immediate difference and, in this way, you should start to build up a feel for what your car does. Obviously, if you do make such major changes to the car, take care in the first couple of laps to ensure that you are not caught out by dramatically changed handling. If you don't notice the difference, the chances are that you need more coaching! Either you are not tuned in to the car, of there may be a fundamental problem elsewhere in the car that is masking the effect of the changes made.

From there, you can be more and more precise about settings until you reach the optimum settings for you and your car at a specific circuit. All of this data must be recorded in your log book, otherwise your efforts will go to waste. Extreme changes during testing should always be made with due caution, but the result should be a far greater understanding of the handling characteristics of your car.

The ride height of the car can have a critical effect on the handling. Most purpose-built racing cars have adjustable ride height and there will usually be a regulation for the class that dictates the minimum ride height for the car in race trim. This is frequently, and very easily, checked by the scrutineers and any car failing the ride height check will be penalised.

A minimum ride height of 40mm is commonly used and the car must meet this minimum at the end of the race with the driver aboard. It is sensible to set the car up before the race with a ride height of around 43mm to allow a safety margin. As the race develops and the dampers get hotter, the car will tend to sink a little and it is quite possible to bend the suspension slightly by hitting a kerb during the race.

Not only should the car be set as low as is sensible, but the weight of the car should be evenly distributed around the four corners. Checking corner weights should become a routine when a racing car is being prepared and some very accurate systems are now available for doing this. Most professional race teams will carry such a system with them to race meetings along with a flat patch for checking the suspension settings.

However, this type of facility will probably be beyond most amateur racers. The same information can be obtained by using a mechanical weight gauge along with three blocks of wood of the same height as the scales at rest. For light-weight racing cars a set of four bathroom scales can even be used. The aim is to have an even weight distribution around the four corners of the car. Obviously, engine position will tend to make one end of the car heavier, but it is important to at least get even weights on the ends of the same axle.

Adjusting corner weights is typically done by lengthening or shortening the springs on particular corners, by either changing springs or adding spacers. It can be something of a process of trial and error but it will be time well spent.

The other important variables around the suspension are to do with the attitude of the wheels. The camber of a wheel is the angle at which the wheel sits in relation to the vertical plane. Standing at the front of the car and looking at the front wheels, if the top edge of the wheel rim is nearer the body of the car than the bottom edge of the rim, that is negative camber. If the bottom of the rim is nearer the body of the car than the top of the rim, that is positive camber. Most racing cars run with some amount of negative camber.

For more information on the effect of camber on your particular type of car, talk to the technicians from the tyre supplier for the class of racing you are contesting. They should be able to give you basic data about how much camber to run on your car.

The castor angle is that at which the suspension uprights stand in relation to the vertical. Changing the castor angle will affect the loading on the steering and you will find the steering gets progressively heavier or lighter as you change the castor angle. The range of options may well be limited by what is available on the car and research in a specialist book is recommended before any major changes are made. Undoubtedly, some people race successfully for many seasons without changing castor angles.

The final normal adjustment in relation to suspension is what is known as toe-in or toe-out. If you stand facing the front of the car, toe-in is when the leading edges of the wheel rims are closer together than the rear edges. If it looks like both front wheels are pointing out, you have toe-out.

The main effect in terms of handling, primarily on a single-seater, is that, if you are running toe-in, as you turn into a corner, the outside tyre is taking the loading and effectively guiding the car. However, this does not necessarily apply to saloon cars. If you are running toe-out, the inside tyre is actually dragging the car in towards the corner. The theory is that toe-out can help counter understeer, but not many drivers actually run their cars with toe-out as a standard set-up. In all cases, it is worth checking further about the right settings for the particular type of car you are racing, as the principals do vary with different types of car.

Most drivers run with toe-in as standard which provides stability on the car. On the rear of the car, you will find that toe-in increases stability, particularly under braking. However, some of the more competitive front-wheel drive racing saloon cars may well run with toe-out on the rear which, effectively, provides a degree of rear-wheel steering. Traditionally, a front-wheel drive saloon will understeer and toe-out on the rear wheels may help with this problem.

5.2 TYRES

Tyres are an immensely important part of motor racing and they will be a considerable element of your racing budget. In all cases, the motorsport division of the tyre manufacturer will be a useful source of information about tyre technology. At higher level race meetings, the major manufacturers will be represented by a supply truck with fitting facilities and tyre engineers will be on hand.

In classes where treaded road tyres are mandatory, you will find most drivers using tyres that have been buffed down to around 3mm of tread. The reason you buff a road tyre is that the tread block is so high when new that it wobbles and makes the car feel unstable. When you buff the tyre down it becomes much more squat. That's why road tyres always feels very good just before you have to change them. Buffing tyres is simply a process of wiping out some of the tread depth on the new tyre.

However, in such a situation you still need newer tyres with around 5mm of tread as wet tyres. If you are very organised, as you wear the tyres, the wets become intermediates and then ultimately your dry tyres.

Slick tyres typically have a 4mm tread depth when new. If the tread is any deeper than that, the tyre will overheat. A slick tyre works by getting hot. Energy from the circuit and sideways loading heats up the rubber, and the tyre won't really work below 50 degrees centigrade. This is the temperature taken at the point where the tread and the carcass of the tyre meet. That is why tyre technicians push the gauges into the tyre and don't just take the surface temperature.

Surface temperatures are a guide but they aren't enough if you really want to know what is going on. Slicks are designed to carry on working at temperatures up to 110 degrees. At 115 degrees a tyre will be getting to the top end of its tolerance. Over this level, the tyre will overheat and start to fail. A simple pyrometer costing under £100 will be sufficient for recording the temperatures and the aim is to get consistent temperatures across the width of the tyre.

A slick tyre will warm up in a lap or two, depending upon the circuit, the car, the type of day and how hard the driver tries. A slick tyre will always give you a quicker lap when it is new and that should show as at least half a second on the stop watch.

However, particularly with a radial construction, a tyre used in this way when later used as a race tyre will tend to drop off more quickly than a tyre that has been conditioned carefully. The best way to condition slick tyres is to do a warm up lap followed by two or three normal laps and then come in and put the tyres to one side. Those tyres will be much more consistent and the drop off in performance will be much less.

Conditioning of new tyres is important, particularly at a circuit like Thruxton where tyres that have gone through a couple of heat cycles will last far better than new tyres put on the for race. If tyres are not conditioned in this way, they will be far more likely to hit problems such as blistering. Ideally, if you have bought new slicks and want to make them last and be as consistent as possible through their life, condition them in this way. Ideally, take them through one heat cycle, leave them a few days and repeat the process.

Try to watch how the tyres are wearing. If you are running a lot of camber on the car you will probably find that you will wear one side out first. Also, if have a lot of understeer, you will tend to wear the outside edge of the tyre. If you are vigilant, you may be able to turn the tyre on the rim, otherwise you will wear one side out and have to throw them away. Most radial racing tyres are not directional.

Always inspect your tyres very carefully after each race for obvious signs of damage. If you have a hot air gun and a paint scraper, it is worth removing the debris from the tyre. This is not taking rubber off, it is simply removing the rubbish that a tyre picks up when it gets hot. This accumulation will stop the tyre working properly. This not only exposes a whole new area of rubber, it also allows a close inspection for cuts, flat-spots and other damage to the tyre. Because of the heat generated by slick tyres, they will easily pick up debris at the end of a race. When you come off the circuit, try and avoid any rough ground or gravel as tyres can be ruined in this way.

A flat-spot on a tyre is created when the wheel locks up under braking and the tread is left on the circuit. A high-speed spin can also lead to flat-spots, sometimes on all four tyres. Once a tyre is flat-spotted it is wrecked. You could carry on using the tyre, but if it locks up again, it will always go back to the first flat-spot.

Over the winter, slick tyres should be stored in a dark, dry area away from electricity and solvents. Tyres should also be kept away from frost if at all possible and kept at a minimum of 5 degrees centigrade. Some of the compounds can start to fracture if dropped when very cold.

If you are in any doubt about the suitability of a tyre, always seek the professional advice of the tyre technicians. At higher level meetings, the major suppliers will have service vehicles on hand with a supply of tyres and fitting technicians. If you are unsure about the age of a tyre, a call to the supplier quoting the reference from the side of the tyre should establish the age and, therefore, the suitability of the tyre for use. No tyre more than five years old should be used.

While slicks are designed to work only when they get hot, wet tyres stop working when they get hot. They have a very different compound to slick tyres and, if the track is starting to dry, the objective is to try and keep the temperature down and you will see drivers going off line to drive through any remaining puddles in this situation. A wet tyre will overheat much more quickly and the blocks of rubber will start to fail.

If in doubt about what tyres to use in changing conditions, seek advice from the tyre experts if they are at the track. They will readily help, and are not simply there to take your money for more tyres.

When you join a particular class of racing, the chances are that there will be a control tyre for the class. If this is the case, that particular type of tyre is mandatory and all cars must use that tyre and no other. Control tyres have many benefits, particularly in helping to make a level playing field. If the choice of tyres is free, there is always the chance that the better-funded drivers will seek out extra-soft compounds to try to gain an advantage. In some of the more professional classes, although there is a control tyre, regulations may specify a limit on the number of tyres any car can use during the course of a meeting. At club level, however, many competitors will expect to race the whole season on one set of tyres.

Tyre pressures have a big effect on the handling of the car. It is important to remember that the more laps you do, the higher the tyre pressure will be as heat build-up will increase the tyre pressure through the race.

Here, the recording of pressures at the end of the race is very important as this will show you how much pressure the tyre has gained during the race.

5.3 AERODYNAMICS

" NUMBER THIRTEEN
THIS IS EAST MIDLANDSAIRPORT-
YOU ARE ENTERING RESTRICTED
AIR SPACE."

DONINGTON PARK

FOLEY

AERODYNAMICS

Like suspension, aerodynamics is a vast subject that is covered fully in books dedicated to the subject. If you are racing a road-going saloon or sports car, it is not a subject you need really be concerned with. However, if you chose to compete in a purpose built sportscar or single seater, it is an area that you will need to understand.

The basics of aerodynamics are the front and rear wings (where fitted to a car) and these are instrumental in deciding how much grip you have at either end of the car. In simple terms, the steeper the angle that the wing

115

is set at, the more grip it will generate. When you hear drivers talk about putting more wing on, they are, in fact, increasing the angle that the wing is set at so that more downforce, and therefore grip, is generated.

If you look at a Grand Prix car at a circuit like Monaco, you will be able to read the sponsors name on the rear wing very easily. This is because the cars are running a good deal of wing to try and stick the back of the car to the track around the twisty track. If you look at the same car at a high-speed circuit like Hockenheim, the wing will be much closer to flat and the sponsors name will be much harder to see! In Indycars, when they are running on the very fast super-speedways, the rear wing is completely flat, as any amount of wing will have a detrimental effect on outright speed.

Any wing setting is a compromise between straight-line speed and grip in the corners. You can never have the ultimate of both and every set-up on a racing car is a balance between those two key factors. You should be prepared to change the settings for every track. However, in the early stages of your learning curve, it can be beneficial to find a set-up that you are comfortable with and stay with it while you learn about the car.

Also, it is worth remembering that a low downforce set-up with minimal rear wing will make the car tricky to control in the corners. This is particularly true of a circuit like Thruxton. While the high-speed nature of the circuit calls for low-drag settings, the trade-off is a lack of grip for the corners. An experienced and talented driver may be able to handle this with ease, but a novice could easily be caught out. Therefore, a safe set-up is one with a reasonable amount of wing even if straight-line speed suffers as a result.

It is safe to say that no-one ever crashed due to lack of straight-line speed, but many have come to grief thanks to minimal downforce through the corners! A place or two lost on the straight is far preferable to a high-speed visit to the under-growth around the sweeping corners at the back of the circuit.

Traditionally, on the trailing edge of the rear wing is a small flap known as the Gurney flap. This flap dictates the airflow over the top of the wing and leads to an increase in low to medium speed downforce as well as an increase in drag.

Front wings, if fitted, will control the amount of grip for the front of the car. If you increase the wing angle at the front of the car, you are effectively increasing the amount of downforce at the front of the car. This will give the front of the car more grip and will also probably make the steering heavier. Normally, this is one way of counter-acting understeer, particularly in medium and high-speed corners.

In low-speed corners such as tight chicanes or hairpin bends, the aerodynamics will have little or no effect as you will not be going fast enough to generate much in the way of downforce. If you have problems with understeer in these corners, you will need to look at the mechanical grip generated by the tyres or suspension for the answer rather than the aerodynamics. Ride height can also effect the amount of mechanical grip a car produces.

On more sophisticated racing cars, the ride height will have a significant effect on the aerodynamics of the car as airflow underneath the car can be as important as airflow over the top of the car. At the front of some cars, notably saloons and sports car, will be a splitter. This forms the leading bottom edge of the bodywork and literally splits the air above and beneath the car. Splitters are also common on racing cars from the period when full-width noses were the norm.

5.4 GEARBOXES AND RATIOS

Gearboxes will, of course, vary from car to car. In road-going type cars you may have a standard production synchromesh gearbox with no option to change the ratios. As can be inherent in production units, the gap between gears, particularly second to third, can be long and cause problems during acceleration. But if that is what you have, you must simply make the best of it and remember that your rivals on the track will probably be similarly constrained. You may then need to consider this when developing your driving style to suit particular circuits.

In single-seater racing, only the entry level Formula EuroFirst category uses a standard production gearbox. All other single-seater classes will have a purpose-built racing gearbox, either with four or five speeds, which will allow gear ratios to be changed. By changing the ratios you can tailor the gears to suit each circuit you visit. For instance, you may have a fourth gear suitable for a top speed of 100mph or one that is good for 120mph.

In simple terms, the gearing you would use for a high-speed track like Thruxton would be very different to the gearing you would use at a tight and twisty track like Cadwell Park. Frequently at race meetings, you will see teams changing gear ratios between qualifying and the race after drivers have found the ratios selected for qualifying to be inappropriate. This is an area that should really be covered during testing, if you have been able to visit the circuit in advance.

Obviously if you change the ratio for one gear, you should probably change the other gears around it so that you maintain as even a spread of power as possible through the gears. The ideal is to avoid a long gap between gears so that acceleration suffers. Also, you ideally want each corner to be nicely in the rev range generated by one gear so that you are not having to try and change gear mid-corner.

On some faster circuits you may only use first gear at the start of the race, although a tight hairpin such as Shaws Corner at Mallory Park will almost certainly be taken in first gear. Much of this will depend on just what ratios you have in your spares kit and you should try and gather information about gearing each time you run the car.

Some standard cars may even perform better if standing starts are taken in second gear. It really is a case of trial and error to find out what is best for your car. In very wet conditions, some cars may be better started in second gear to counter the possibility of excess wheelspin.

What you need to try and avoid is running out of revs in top gear before you reach the end of the main straight. Once again Thruxton offers up a rather unique scenario as many drivers find themselves up against the rev limiter during the long flat-out drag from Church back towards the Chicane. Having the correct ratios for the circuit can be an advantage if you are battling with a car of similar performance, as you may have better acceleration out of a corner, for instance.

For more information, always speak to the manufacturer of the gearbox, who should also be able to supply you with charts for working out the correct ratios. If in doubt, and it can be a confusing area to the inexperienced, don't be afraid to enlist the help of more experienced racers in your category.

Increasingly in the higher levels of the sport, sequential and semi-automatic gearboxes are being used. The potential advantage of a sequential gearbox is that you can make faster gear-changes, simply by pushing the lever away from you or pulling it towards you, to go up and down the box as appropriate. The system is like that used on a motorbike and the chances of missing changes are reduced. The down-side is that you have to go through each gear in turn when coming down through the box under braking for a corner.

With a normal H-pattern gearbox, you can often change from fifth straight into third gear when changing down for a corner, and avoid going through fourth. The down-change will be accompanied by a process called heel and toe, which is a skill you need to learn at the racing school.

When you brake for a corner and depress the clutch, you move the gear lever into neutral and, at the same moment, roll your right foot across onto the throttle and match the engine revs to the road speed as you then go on into the lower gear. During this process, you still maintain the same amount of braking pressure with your right foot. Once mastered, it will become a natural process and it is vital to learn this as early as possible. You can practice it in your road car! If you do not heel and toe, letting the clutch out suddenly could cause the rear wheels to lock under braking with a rear wheel drive car.

Another term you may come across is short-shifting. This is when you change up at less than the normal revs. The reason for doing this may be that you have a problem with the car, that you are in a longer race and are conserving the car or that the track is slippery from rain and you want to avoid the risk of losing traction with high revs. Also, if there is a sequence of corners on the track that come in quick succession, you may need to short-shift out of one corner so that you are ready for the next one. If you run through a corner at peak revs, the car will tend to be less stable.

Power-shifting is also used in some types of racing car. Here, the driver changes gear without coming off the power but this is only for the very rich! Though not really recommended at club level, it is something you can do, depending upon the car. Gearbox specialists say that is does tend to wear the dog-rings and gear ratios in the gearbox excessively because you are not allowing the gearbox the correct time to select the next gear. Be warned; it is very easy to over-rev engines during power-shifting and we do not recommend it for amateur racers!

Being able to change gear smoothly and precisely is a skill that can produce benefit on the stop-watch. Also, that smoothness and precision can show further benefits in the size of your bills for gearbox rebuilds! When you have that rebuild done, the specialist can tell you whether you are doing it right or wrong by looking at the way the gears are worn. They will probably tell you what you are doing wrong from the internal damage.

5.5 DATA-LOGGING

Data-logging systems used to be the preserve of the well-funded professional teams. However, nowadays, even the most humble of club racing car may be equipped with some form of electronic data gathering system. A data-logging system is a piece of electronic hardware that is installed in your race car and accompanied by analysis software that is installed on a personal computer.

Before you decide to buy a system, take a look at the dash layout offered by that system and try and visualise how that would look in your particular car. Each of the systems on the market have a different way of placing information on the display and some may be more suitable to your car than others.

The most common information that drivers have on the display are engine revs, miles per hour, water temperature, oil pressure and temperature, battery voltage and fuel pressure. These are typically the basics that you would expect to get from a data-logging system. Not only will you be able to read this information at a glance during the race, but afterwards you can down-load it to a computer, preferably a lap-top, and study the information.

DATA LOGGING

Some systems also include the facility to pre-programme alarm warnings. For instance, if the oil pressure drops below a pre-set minimum, a warning light and descriptive message can be displayed.

Other useful information that will particularly help with finding where you are losing time during a lap will cover things like throttle and brake positions. Of course, if you have such a system, there is no place to hide! But if you are honest with yourself, the data you gain may well highlight exactly where you need to improve to match the class pacesetters.

In the European Formula Palmer Audi single-seater class, where all the cars are prepared and run centrally, all drivers get a data trace after each run in the car. This is over-laid with the trace of the fastest driver in the session and so the driver can immediately identify where he is losing time, and why.

Most of the modern systems are very user-friendly and the supplier will be able to help you get started. Of course, there is always the temptation to get a system because everyone else has got one, so be sure that are going to gain benefit from it before parting with valuable funds.

A very important element, which is often integral, is a lap timer which will give you an instant read-out of the lap you have just completed. More advanced systems can provide a wealth of information from a host of sensors that can be attached to various components. Damper movement, suspension loadings and ride height measurements can all be pulled in to give you a very comprehensive picture of what the car is doing at every point on the lap.

If you are really serious, especially about qualifying, another useful facility is the running lap display. This can tell you throughout a hot lap how much you are up on the previous best at any point on the lap. In classes where tyre performance is critical over a limited number of laps, this could save a driver pressing on with a lap that should have been aborted!

If full data-logging is beyond your budget or your needs, a simple hot-lap system can be bought. This in-car display links to a transmitter placed on the pit wall to give a read-out of the lap just completed. At under £300, the hot-lap system can give you instant access to accurate lap times.

Telemetry systems, widely used in Grand Prix racing, can analyse what is going on while the car is on the track and communicate that information back to the pits. Regulations prohibit changes being made to the car from the pits, however! But for most racers, some form of data-logging will be more than sufficient.

Chapter 6
So you need a sponsor!

IN THIS CHAPTER

6.1 A TWO-WAY BUSINESS DEAL
  - ➤ The return
  - ➤ Business, not charity
  - ➤ Brand awareness

6.2 MAKING THE PITCH
  - ➤ Selecting the targets
  - ➤ The proposal
  - ➤ Selling yourself
  - ➤ Non-financial support

6.3 MAKING IT WORK FOR BOTH PARTIES
  - ➤ Off-track opportunities
  - ➤ At the race meeting
  - ➤ Tell it like it is!
  - ➤ Sponsor hunters

6.4 KEEPING THEM INTERESTED

➤ Team information

➤ Press releases

➤ Making the announcement

➤ When, where and how to announce

6.5 CORPORATE HOSPITALITY

➤ Where and when?

➤ The costs

➤ Meeting the guests

➤ Team tours

6.1   A TWO-WAY BUSINESS DEAL

A TWO-WAY BUSINESS DEAL

Sponsorship. An arrangement where a company gives you an amount of money, you put their stickers on your racing car and go off and have a good time. Incredibly, some drivers still see it this way. If this is your view of sponsorship, you are going to fail. A sponsorship deal is a two-way business deal. Nothing more, nothing less.

How do I get sponsorship? That is one of the most common questions that hopeful newcomers ask at racing schools. To try to shed a little light on the subject, we have included this chapter. But we do not claim to have all the answers and can only provide some pointers and commonsense. To really succeed at sponsor-hunting, you should seek out books that concentrate solely on the subject.

It is a fact of life that many budding drivers cannot afford to compete at the level at which they wish to, simply through lack of finances. Not everyone is fortunate enough to either have family money to spend or a business of their own to fund their sport. If you have either of these, you can probably skip the rest of this chapter and get on with your racing plans.

But those lucky souls are few and far between and most people starting racing will be doing so from their own hard-earned funds. In such a situation, thoughts of sponsorship will undoubtedly surface. But stop and think for a moment. If you cannot even manage your first season of racing from your own resources, are you the manna from heaven that a company with money to spend has been searching for?

I recently received a sponsorship bid from a hopeful youngster. It told me all about his potential, his racing school activities and which championship he was going to win with my money. However, when I dug deeper into the meandering four-page letter, it dawned on me that this chap had not even competed in his first race.

If you are a complete novice, I suggest you forget about sponsorship during your debut season. First, you will probably be so busy that looking after a sponsor will be a demand that you will struggle to meet. Second, how much better it looks if you have some proven pedigree of results to show when you start knocking on doors. Of course, if a sponsor falls into your lap during your first season, don't turn them away!

Before you even start thinking about approaching companies, you must understand a fundamental about sponsorship. It is not charity. It is a business deal. To stand a chance of winning sponsorship from a company, you must be able to demonstrate that the amount of money you are asking them to spend, will be at least matched, and preferably exceeded, by the value you will return to them.

It is not easy to quantify the value of the return, but it must be a central part of your bid. Without it, your proposal is likely to reach the bin within a few seconds of arriving through the letter box. Put yourself in the position of the marketing director at the target company. If the potential value of the return matches or exceeds the cost of the sponsorship, you might just be interested. If the bid is a thinly-disguised request for charity, you will not spend much time reaching a decision.

So how do you go about ensuring that your proposal stands a chance of success? There is, of course, no simple answer to this, but try and look at what a company may want to get from a sponsorship arrangement.

Brand awareness is central to most marketing programmes. A great deal of advertising and a lot of sponsorship is aimed at increasing brand awareness. The company will be seeking to imprint its name and identity into the memories of the audience so that, when a potential customer makes a buying decision, they will think of company X first.

Quantifying the value of this is not easy, but you should be considering several areas where your programme can increase brand awareness. Typically, this can be through raceday crowds, TV coverage and media exposure. Your decision about which series to contest may be influenced by potential TV coverage if that is central to your sponsorship deal.

Corporate entertainment is very big business and is a major part of motorsport sponsorship. Many companies use race meetings as an opportunity to entertain clients (past, present and future). Motor racing is an exciting sport and a day at a race meeting is an ideal way of developing relationships with clients and building customer loyalty. If their car is battling for the lead of the race, it adds to the enjoyment of the customers.

The third reason for sponsorship is of a more philanthropic nature. It is possible that the managing director of a company is a motor racing enthusiast and sponsors a driver primarily for the opportunity to become involved in the sport. However, these arrangements are relatively rare and often come about due to a personal link between the driver and the sponsor. So, if your favourite uncle has a successful business, make sure you visit him regularly!

The bottom line of any proposal must be that it can deliver benefit to the company that equals or exceeds the value of the sponsorship that you are seeking. If the two amounts do not tally, you are either asking for too much, or giving too little back. Or both!

To coin a well-known expression, you could say that gaining sponsorship is 95% perspiration and 5% inspiration. Those that are good at getting sponsorship will tell you that good homework and determination are essential, and that you just have to keep trying. It's not easy, but why should it be?

6.2 MAKING THE PITCH

MAKING A PITCH

We have all heard horror stories of hopeful drivers sending out 500 letters requesting sponsorship and getting three replies that all said no. Using the shot-gun approach of firing at random in the hope of hitting something is most unlikely to reap any rewards and will probably leave you disillusioned.

You have to be more scientific when planning which companies to target. Time spent researching possible targets will save a lot of wasted effort and expense. It is far better to make a bid to 20 likely targets than 500 chosen seemingly at random from the Yellow Pages. But how do you find out who to target?

First of all, consider the scale of your racing activity and the likely benefits you are going to be able to offer. Grand Prix teams have substantial marketing divisions which are focused on finding multi-million pound targets. Extensive research and forward planning goes into any proposal made and the bid will be very finely tailored to suit the aspirations of the target company.

At your level, it may all seem rather different but you should aim to use the same principals. If you are contesting a club-level championship in a road-going car, you are wasting your time approaching major blue-chip companies. They will be besieged by sponsorship proposals from all types of sports and leisure activity, and unless you have something remarkable about your bid, they will have seen and heard it all before.

Think about the audience that you can deliver a message to. A company specialising in chairlifts for the elderly is unlikely to be very interested in a motorsport programme. However, a company with an obvious interest in attracting a youthful audience (motorsport gets the most attention from males in the 18-40 age range) may be more appropriate.

Consider the geographic area that will interest your target. If the company has a strong local market, you may need to consider how well you can service that need if contesting a national championship. Study your local press, particularly the business pages, and keep an eye out for companies that are expanding or developing new product lines. They may be more interested in your proposal than a company fighting to survive by making staff redundant.

Of course, there is no better way of researching than by tapping up friends and relatives. Most will be employed in some way, and may be able to point you at suitable companies. Look at who is doing the major advertising locally. If they have an advertising budget, they may have something for marketing or the right sponsorship opportunity.

All of these ways, and others, will help you compile a list of likely targets that seem to match what you have to offer. It may take many months to build up your target list but it is worth doing it carefully. Then, your proposal needs to be presented in good time. Don't send out letters in February hoping to find backing for the season that is about to start. Most budgets are set in the autumn and so you should try and time your bid accordingly.

The next stage is to pinpoint the target recipient at the company. Simply addressing your bid to the company is asking for it to find the bin. You need to establish who to send it to, and this will probably be a marketing manager or, in a smaller company, the managing director. Whichever, make sure it is personally addressed.

Ideally, your proposal should be mailed to the appropriate person and then followed up with a telephone call a few days later. This will allow you to check that the bid has reached the correct person, answer any questions and, hopefully, pitch for a meeting for further discussion.

That all sounds quite easy, but if your proposal is good enough to get you through the front door of the company, then it has been a success. After that, it is down to you to sell yourself and the concept to the decision-makers.

So what should you include in your proposal? Once again, there is no golden formula for success. But, consider that the average mailshot is only glanced at for a few seconds before being consigned to the bin by a busy manager. If you are to get anywhere, your proposal needs to create an immediate impression and make the reader want to look further. If the first thing that the reader sees is an A4 page crammed full of small print, you are probably doomed.

If you have done your homework properly, you will have identified the corporate colours and identity of the company. With the wide availability of computer drawing packages, why not create a colour impression of your car with the company logo already in place? If you cannot do it yourself, you probably know someone who can and even if you have to pay for it to be done, it could just be worth the effort. This stands more chance of grabbing the attention of a marketing manager than pages and pages of prose.

So, that could form the front cover of your bid. You will, of course, need to tailor each copy of your bid to the recipient, but proper research will have produced a small target list anyway. In the following pages of the proposal, you will need some words about you, your car, your plans and what you expect to provide in return for support.

Don't go on for pages and pages, and don't cram each page full of words. Emphasise the potential benefits available to the company. This should be a very prominent part of the bid! It is questionable as to whether to include figures at this stage. Most experts say not, keep that until you have reached the stage of a meeting.

Keep the initial proposal fairly simple and punchy, something that can be read and digested in less than five minutes. Four or five pages of A4 should be plenty. Your trusty PC should be able to create clean, nicely laid-out pages and the use of photographs is always a good idea.

But, for goodness sake, if you are going to send photos, don't use a muddy shot from a rainy Cadwell Park with not a spectator in sight! Make sure the photos are from a bright day, with (ideally) you leading a group of cars, and with a crowd in the background. Try and convey the excitement of the sport in the photograph.

Include details of how to contact you should they require further information. Ideally, include a daytime telephone number and if you use a number with an answering machine, make sure the message is clean and polite. A sponsor-hunter recently sent out a mailshot to prospective backers inviting them to call a certain number. Had you called that number, the answering machine message went along the lines of: 'Leave a message if you like, we might get back to you but we probably won't'. That's okay if it's only the mother-in-law who is likely to call, but a potential sponsor would probably have hung up there and then.

Should you be lucky enough to be invited to a meeting, your bid now enters a new phase. This is where you really have to sell yourself and many people are not comfortable with this. The best thing to do is to treat this something like a job interview. Get the suit out of the wardrobe, get the oil off your hands and be professional. Don't be too modest about your own abilities and potential, but don't over-sell yourself or your programme either. Be honest and up-beat. Show your enthusiasm for the sport and your own plans.

If you have done your research, you should be able to talk comfortably about the company, its products and any recent changes such as new products or services. Take with you any more background information about the sport, including statistics like number of spectators, TV audiences, details of other local companies involved in sponsorship, and so on. There is no substitute to being prepared. Some of the higher profile championships employ media officers who will have much of this information at their finger tips. If that is the case, make good use of them.

An important opportunity that some people seem to overlook in the quest for money, is to pitch for non-financial support. There are many ways in which backing in terms of parts, facilities and other services can make a useful contribution to your costs while not being a major financial burden to the backer. The fact that you may not be asking for cash support may be far more attractive to a company and, of course, such backers can make excellent subsidiary sponsors for your programme.

Should you, after all this, be able to agree backing, you will probably need some form of agreement with the company. A letter of understanding is a recommended minimum in which you spell out exactly what has been agreed and what each party is going to get from the association. It is imperative that there are no misunderstandings at this stage, as they will only become big problems as the season develops. If the amounts of money are substantial, you will probably need to have a formal contract drawn up. If this is so, it is vital to take professional legal advice.

6.3 MAKING IT WORK FOR BOTH PARTIES

In reality, success on the track is not central to a successful sponsorship deal. Obviously, the driver will want to do as well as possible and race and class wins are good opportunities to promote the sponsor. But a good sponsorship deal will involve much more than just going out and racing at weekends.

Just what goes on around the racing programme to promote the sponsor and its involvement will largely be dictated by the scale of investment and the sponsor's business activities. However, there are a number of things which can be done to benefit the company and start providing the all-important pay-back that the sponsor will want to see.

This list gives some suggestions, but is in no way definitive:

- **Use of the car for displays, conferences, product launches and showroom promotions.**
- **Use of the driver for company events such as sales conferences.**
- **Car on display at company headquarters or in showrooms.**
- **Use of car at public events like county shows and exhibitions.**
- **Use of the racing programme for sales competitions and customer incentives.**
- **Use of the racing programme for staff competitions and incentives.**
- **Use of the racing programme in advertising campaigns.**
- **Customer entertainment at race meetings.**
- **Customer activity days at racing schools using the racing programme as a focus.**
- **Staff incentive days at race meetings.**

There are many other ways to link a racing programme to the sponsor's business and these will need to discussed during preliminary meetings. However, if you can provide some of the above, you will be ahead of the people who simply want to take the money and go racing.

Now, of course, going racing is what it is all about. You may argue that you are a racing driver and need to focus on the racing programme rather than things like the Managing Director's local garden fete. It is true that the needs of the racing must be a priority, but it is the peripheral activities that can really make a difference.

So, what do you do if you are busy trying to run the racing programme and the demands of the sponsor are encroaching increasingly upon your time? The answer depends upon just how much the sponsor is spending. If it is a substantial sum, you are going to need to enlist support, either paid or voluntary, to take on some of the workload to leave you time to meet the sponsor's needs. After all, you probably agreed to them at the start of the deal, so you have a duty to see it through.

If the deal is big enough, you may have to prepare a second, but identical, car in the sponsor's colours if a busy schedule of showroom displays and exhibitions means that you are not going to be left with enough time to prepare the car properly and go testing.

Bigger sponsors frequently have a second car to use in these circumstances. This may be last year's car or, perhaps, a show car that need not be prepared to the same standard as the race car. But, if your deal is modest - and it probably will be - you will need to juggle dates to satisfy both sides of the arrangement.

The next thing to agree with your sponsors is what involvement they want at the race meetings. Once again, this varies tremendously across the sport. At the top level are the bigger-spending sponsors who use each race meeting to entertain dozens of guests in lavish surroundings. At the other extreme are sponsors who just want to come along and get involved at races, perhaps even helping with the car. Then, there are sponsors who aren't particularly interested in even coming to the races. The important thing is to know what your sponsor wants on race days.

See Chapter 6.5

As a minimum, make sure that your sponsor is invited to each meeting and that, if he wishes to attend, circuit entry tickets are available. It is also worth making sure they have details of the raceday timetable and an idea of where to go to find you when they arrive at the circuit. A nice touch is to write to them before each race with these details and an invitation to attend.

However, be wary of not over-selling the meeting. If the sponsor turns up at Silverstone for a Saturday club meeting in March expecting something close to the Grand Prix, he will be disappointed. Tell it like it is, otherwise you could have some explaining to do on raceday! It is also worth stressing to your sponsor that race circuits are invariably cold and windy. If his wife arrives at the meeting in high-heels expecting glamorous surroundings, and leaves cold, wet and muddy, guess who is going to hear about it all the way home!

All of this may make it seem as though sponsorship is more trouble than it is worth. Certainly, if you were doing all of the above, you would probably have a big-budget backer and a support crew to match. If you are getting a few hundred pounds from a local business, much of this is not appropriate. However, if you set out to delight your sponsor throughout the season, you have a far better chance of retaining his support, perhaps at a higher level, in future seasons.

Finally, on the subject of finding sponsors, there are some individuals and organisations who will try and secure backing on your behalf. As in any field, some are good, some not so good. If you decide to look at this route, be very clear about what you are going to get and what they are going to keep from any backing they secure for you.

6.4 KEEPING THEM INTERESTED

It is a constant source of amazement that some drivers find sponsorship, go off racing and only make contact with the sponsor when, either the money has run out, or, the time has come to ask for another season's support. If this is how you treat sponsors, do not expect to keep them for very long.

Keeping a sponsor informed about your racing must be an essential part of your planning. If you cannot do it for yourself, then find someone to do it for you, and pay them if you have to. I suggest that, if you have been racing on Sunday, your sponsor should have a fax on his desk at 9am Monday morning telling him about the race. Yes, I know you have to drive home from the circuit in time to get to the pub before closing time, and then get up and go to work on Monday morning. But if you cannot find the time to keep your sponsor up to date, you will probably lose him.

135

Your report should be no more than one side of A4 paper, ideally carrying the team name and logo. It should carry basic information about the race meeting, including date, venue and which round of the championship you were contesting. The report should set the scene for the race meeting, detail how you got on in qualifying, how the race went and conclude with the date and venue of the next race. Include some quotes from the driver to add some colour, but strictly avoid any dodgy language.

It need not be brilliantly written, but needs to make sense and portray your racing in a positive light. If you have had problems at the meeting, be honest, but don't resort to slagging off your opponents. Try and produce it on a PC that has a spell-check facility so that you can check it before sending it. Also, try and get someone else to read it before you send it, so that they can check that it makes sense. Proof-reading your own work is the best way to miss errors.

If you haven't got a fax machine, seriously consider investing in one. You don't need to have a separate telephone line, just buy a fax that has an in-built switching system so that you plug it into your normal telephone socket. Once you have one, you will wonder how you ever managed without it!

Increasingly, teams and drivers are using e-mail to distribute information. If you are hooked up to e-mail, you can generate a mailing list of recipients for your press releases and distribute them quickly and easily without the need for a fax machine or stamps and envelopes.

When you have written your sponsor's report, it is very easy to turn this into a press release that you can send to your local papers and radio stations. Part of any successful sponsorship programme will be keeping local media interested and informed about the progress of the Bloggs Toiletries Racing Team. A one-page release faxed to them on Monday morning after the latest race is the best way of trying to ensure local exposure for your sponsor.

Don't forget that your sponsor may have trade magazines for his particular industry that may be able to carry team news. By sending the press release to Toiletries Illustrated you may generate valuable exposure for your sponsor in a publication read by his customers. Equally, your sponsor may wish to have the report sent to important customers, associate companies or branch offices. Of course, if the list grows you could be very busy on a Monday morning, and if the project gets too big, look around for professional help.

This same fax or e-mail list should be used when you first announce the sponsorship deal. However, this may need to be a mailshot as it is best to include photographs from the launch. The press launch is, ideally, the kick-off point for your promotional programme. Normally this will be done sometime before the start of the season and should be planned to generate as much pre-season exposure as possible.

There are many ways of handling a press launch. The Grand Prix teams make it into an art-form but a personal appearance from the Spice Girls may be outside your budget. However, with a little thought, you could come up with a way of getting the picture into the local papers. Try and do something different to the standard photo of the racing car outside the sponsors premises with you grinning inanely while shaking hands with the MD.

The use of a local celebrity in the launch photo will give you a better chance. Why not try the local MP or mayor? They usually love to get their picture in the press for just about any reason, and a successful local business supporting a racing programme should be enough to get them along. You only need them for five minutes to get the photograph taken, perhaps with them sitting in the car. When you have got the relevant number of prints done, make sure you caption them on the reverse for the benefit of the editors.

Choose the location of the photo shoot carefully. Think about the sponsor's area of business and try and link it to the photo. Outside Bloggs Retail in the High Street on Saturday morning could be a good way of getting a crowd scene, but don't forget to check with the council before you do it!

Aside from the initial press launch and post-event reports, try and spot other opportunities for press releases or sponsor bulletins. If there is a gap in the calendar mid-season, try to find an angle for a release. Perhaps you have had a particularly successful test day, or carried out some modifications to the car. By doing this, you should be able to keep the racing programme firmly in the mind of the sponsor, his customers and the local media. And, always send your press releases to the specialist motorsport press. If you are competing in a fairly lowly series, don't expect too much coverage, but there is no harm in trying.

Another nice touch for sponsors, and one that need not cost you very much to do, is to present them with a framed photograph of the car during the season. Motor racing photographers sell their work around the paddock at most race meetings and a good shot of your car, with the sponsor's name nice and clear, makes an ideal present for the sponsor. Better still, get it framed and then it will probably find its way into the boardroom or reception.

If you are successful with your media campaign, try and get cuttings of any reports of your racing activities and keep them in a presentation file. This is a good record of achievement for your sponsor and could be very useful when you meet to discuss the forthcoming season. Even if your current sponsor does not continue, the file will be a handy tool for discussions with potential alternative backers.

More and more race teams and drivers are using websites as marketing and promotional tools. If you have a sponsor, you really should consider getting a website developed and promoting its address through your racing. As a minimum, it should include details of the team, driver, car, sponsor and championship contested.

It should have a photo gallery, preferably with downloadable images for use by local media. But watch out for infringing the copyright of the person who took the photos. Each race should be reported in some way, along with other news and developments. If your sponsor has a website, make sure there is a prominent link both ways.

But the biggest responsibility in having a website is to keep it up to date. If people visit it and find it several weeks out of date, they are unlikely to return. Motor sport is constantly changing, and your website must keep pace.

6.5 CORPORATE HOSPITALITY

Some would argue that corporate hospitality is the scourge of modern sport. But, if they stopped and thought for a while, they might see that without it, modern sport would probably be in a very sorry state. Of course, if you have paid £100 to get into the British Grand Prix as a true enthusiast, you may well look down your nose at the corporate guests who are helicoptered in, wined and dined and watch the first five laps of the race before wandering off for more champagne.

COME ON CHAPS – OR WE'LL MISS THE SECOND RACE.

CORPORATE HOSPITALITY

But without the commercial backing that goes hand in hand with corporate hospitality, motor sport would be dreadfully short of backing. If you attract any substantial amount of sponsorship, you are going to have to get involved in it to some degree.

At the top of the tree, and top of the spenders, are the companies who hire elaborate facilities (permanent or temporary) in which to wine and dine their important guests at a race meeting. Many organisations are expert at providing all the facilities and catering that is required but you are unlikely to see much change from £100 per head for such a day.

At some of the more established circuits, permanent hospitality suites are available either for the full season or for individual meetings. Silverstone, Brands Hatch and Donington have the greatest number of such units and some sponsors will pick one meeting a year at which to entertain their guests.

If your sponsor opts for this type of activity, you will need to be involved. If it is done on a large scale, the providers of the facility will handle much of the work along with all the catering. However, you should then make arrangements with the sponsor to visit the suite at suitable times during the day to meet his guests and talk about the racing. These visits must, of course, be fitted in around the racing timetable. A good time to meet the guests is while lunch is served and you will probably need to stand up and talk to the group about your racing.

Then, soon after the race, the guests will probably want to meet you again to hear all about the race from the inside. You may not feel like doing this, but it is an important responsibility and is a superb way for your sponsor to build relationships with his guests. There is nothing like being able to shake hands with the race winner for sending corporate guests away happy.

During the meeting, the guests will probably want to come and see the team in the paddock. Just what facilities you have to offer will depend upon the scale of your operation. Bigger teams will have transporters and awnings and so a group of guests can be introduced to the team and shown around the racing car. The timing and numbers of such visits need to be slotted into the timetable, but this is another excellent way of making the guests feel involved. If they have children with them, try to arrange to get the kids into the racing car to have their photograph taken. Never under-estimate the influence of children on parent's decision making!

This is all well and good if you have a big budget backer who wants to spend considerable sums on corporate hospitality. But the whole thing can be done on a lesser scale for those on a smaller budget. Modest catering from under the team awning may be appropriate for a smaller number of guests while still giving them the chance to get close to the team.

Finally, a word of warning about when to invite guests. If you are only going to invite sponsors guests to a handful of meetings, choose these meetings very carefully. Geography is, of course, important. Try to pick the circuits that are convenient for most people or close to major customers. Then, try to find out from the race organisers what the timetable for the meeting will be. If your race is the last on a nine or ten-race programme, it is not the ideal meeting for guests. The last races of the day are likely to run after 5pm and, by then, many people will be wanting to head for home.

If you can, plan your guest days for those meetings where you are racing in the first half of the programme. Hanging around until 6.15pm on a cold and wet afternoon to see a shortened race in gathering gloom is not the best way to inspire guests!

CHAPTER 7
BRITISH RACING CATEGORIES

IN THIS CHAPTER

7.1   SALOON CAR CATEGORIES
- ➢ The complete listing of saloon car categories
- ➢ From Touring Cars to 2CVs
- ➢ Background information
- ➢ Current state of health

7.2   SINGLE-SEATER CATEGORIES
- ➢ The complete listing of single-seater categories
- ➢ From Formula 3 to Formula Vee
- ➢ Background information
- ➢ Current state of health

7.3   SPORTS CAR CATEGORIES
- ➢ The complete listing of sports car categories
- ➢ From GT to kit cars
- ➢ Background information
- ➢ Current state of health

7.4   BRITISH RACING CHAMPIONSHIPS
- ➢ The definitive list of British championships
- ➢ Organising club details
- ➢ Cost details
- ➢ Suitable for novices?
- ➢ Slicks or treaded tyres?

7.1 SALOON CAR CATEGORIES

TOURING CARS

The big one, in terms of saloon car racing, for 2-litre Super Touring cars. Big crowds, TV coverage and works teams. Underwent a major overhaul for the 2001 season, with the former high-tech cars replaced by a new generation of touring cars in a less exotic state of development.

The other major change for 2001 was the inclusion of the Super Production category into the overall BTCC scheme. Formerly raced in the National Saloon Championship, the Super Productions cars in the UK run to regulations broadly the same as those used by the FIA. Fro 2001, these cars will run as the Production element of the BTCC, with the new Super Touring cars simply being known as the Touring element.

Neither series is cheap, although the Production cars can be run competitively for between £50,000 and £75,000.

RENAULT CLIO

For 2000, Renault returned to one-make saloon car racing by introducing a 2-litre version of the latest Clio onto the TOCA package. Teams and drivers quickly got behind the new 170bhp racer and it became a major support act to the BTCC in its first season. Slick racing tyres and sequential gearboxes give the Clios a racing appeal.

FORD FIESTA

Ford has been a long-time supporter of one-make saloon car racing, and the latest version of the Fiesta Si was set to be confirmed on the PowerTour package for 2001 as this book went to print. Goods grid and frenetic racing are the hallmark. Though relatively standard, the cars run on slick racing tyres.

Earlier versions of the racing Fiesta find a home in several club-level classes. The Si model (used in the TOCA package until the end of 1996) has a national series although support in 2000 was patchy. The popular XR2 is still raced in both in a championship based in the north-west of England and in a Scottish XR championship. Running in tandem to the north-west based XR2 series is a class for mildly-modified Escort XR3i models.

ASCAR

New for 2001, and taking advantage of the creation of the Rockingham oval, is the Ascar Championship for the American-built racing saloons. This will be Britain's answer to NASCAR racing and the calendar will also include rounds at the Lausitzring in Germany. With the cars costing around £35,000 ready to go, support has been very strong and the series looks like being an immediate hit. However, it is certainly not a series for novices!

PROTON COUPE

The Proton-supported one-make series for Proton Coupes has struggled to gain significant support since it was launched for the 1998 season. At the time of writing its continued existence as a stand-alone series was in question and a home in the Super Coupe Cup was on the cards for 2001.

MINIS

Mini racing has survived with massive competitor support while other classes have come and gone. Under the guidance of the Mini Seven Racing Club, the two classes remain as popular as ever with drivers and spectators. The 1300cc Miglia class is for slick-tyred racers with more powerful engines than the 1000cc Sevens which race on treaded tyres. Superb value for money racing, particularly in the Sevens, makes Mini racing the perfect place for newcomers to start competing. Created in 1997, the Mighty Mini series gained significant support as a great entry-level class for standard 1300i Mini Coopers and by the end of 1999 had gained so much support that it spawned a big brother for 2000. A Super Series allowed drivers to upgrade and gain some more power and some suspension mods, leaving the existing series as a mainly entry-level category.

PICKUPS

Popular with drivers and fans is the Pickup Truck category for 2-litre race-engined spaceframe specials with fibreglass pickup bodies. Famed for fast and furious racing, with many former oval racers in the field, the Pickups are set for an excellent year in 2001 as part of the TOCA package of racing.

LEGENDS

These are 5/8th scale replicas of 1930s American racing saloons powered by 125bhp Yamaha engine. The Legends, available at £10,000 complete, are ideal for newcomers and enjoyed record levels of support in 2000. A Scottish based series for the cars was added during 2000.

EUROCARS

Formerly run as part of the Eurocar package, the series for V8 and V6 racing saloons have enjoyed some very good seasons. However, support dwindled somewhat in 2000 and numbers dropped badly in the V8 class. A revival plan was put in place, lead by Team Brask, to encourage more drivers to race in the category. The V6 Mondeo-based spaceframe racers continue to produce close racing, with many of the drivers having stepped up from oval racing.

MODIFIED RACING SALOONS

Formula Saloon provides a home for powerful and well-developed saloon cars but rules have been written to keep out the more out-landish creations that ultimately led to the demise of Thundersaloons. Former Touring Cars are becoming increasingly popular in the 2-litre class. The Modified Production Saloon class allows considerable engine, brake and suspension development over the original production car, but less so than in Formula Saloons. For 2000 the ModProd were wedded to the Super Road Saloon series to create one championship with stronger grids.

Roughly tied in with Super Road Saloon regs is the Castle Combe Saloon Car Cup along with the Scottish Road Saloon series and a Lydden Hill-based championship. The Castle Combe series is one of the most successful of all, with capacity grids and excellent racing.

The Ford Saloon class can overlap with ModProds, but, as the title suggests, is only for cars bearing the blue oval. As well as the Cosworth monsters, many XR2 and Escort models find a good home in the Ford Saloon class.

CLASSIC AND HISTORIC SALOONS

At the top of the tree for those wanting to compete in period racing saloons is the Classic Thunder category. The class is for the type of car raced in the BTCC of the 1960s, as well as cars seen in special saloon racing in more recent times, but still with original chassis. The series is also home for the Group 2 and Group 5 machinery of the 1970s.

Away from Classic Thunder, the Classic Saloon Car Club has three categories covering a 25-year period starting with pre 1960 models. Now well in decline, the Classic Saloon class (Pre '60) runs with the Historic Saloons (Pre '66). Modifications are kept well in check to ensure that the cars remain in period racing trim.

Moving up an era, is the CSCC Post Historic Class (Pre 74) where the Dolomite Sprints and early Capris have a ball, while many of them also contest the Group 1 Touring Car series for the type of cars that contested the BTCC in the early 80s. In all cases, the Classic Saloon Car Club is a good place to start if you want to race a period saloon with modest modifications in a friendly environment that helps novices.

Last but not least in terms of racing saloons with history is the Historic Racing Saloon Register series. Effectively, this was an off-shoot of the Classic Touring Car movement instigated by competitors concerned at the cost of the cars being developed for the series. Regulations are rather tighter and the cars race in similar trim to their counterparts of the 1960s. Now aligned to the HSCC, the series has enjoyed strong support in the last couple of years.

ROAD SALOONS

From humble beginnings when conceived by Tim Dodwell, the Road Saloon movement has thrived on providing low cost saloon racing. As the title suggests, the Road Saloon class is for genuine road-going cars that must have current MOT certificates and be driven to, and hopefully from, the circuit. That alone limits modifications and carefully controlled rules ensure that the most mods that are done are for safety reasons. There is no better place to start racing with a modest budget!

HOT AND STOCK HATCHES

In recent seasons, the 750 Motor Club has added to the opportunity for drivers looking to race in near-standard cars by introducing the highly successful Hot Hatch championship. Once again cars must have a current MOT certificate and a 1600cc capacity limit means that it is all about cheap to run tin-tops. So successful has the Hot Hatch series been that a further class, called Stock Hatch, was added which keeps the cars even closer to standard specification. Incredibly popular, this is one of the very best starting points for newcomers.

LOW COST ONE-MAKE SALOONS

At the highest level one-make saloon car racing can be pretty expensive. However, further down the racing spectrum, drivers are having enormous fun for a fraction of the cost in a host of single-model or single-marque championships.

The BMW Challenge which, as you might expect, caters for any production model BMW. Fairly extensive tuning can be done so this is not the cheapest of the classes for those at the sharp end of the field. One half of the BARC/MG Owners Club racing championship is for front-wheel drive MG saloons and a host of Maestros and Montegos with minimal modifications provide excellent value for money racing. The other half of the class is for MG sports cars.

If Alfa Romeos are your first love, the Alfa Romeo Owners' Club promotes an excellent championship for Alfas in varying stages of modification and the series is so popular that it has two races per meeting. A bonus for Alfa racers is that they can also contest the AutoItalia series for any Italian car. A few Lancias, some Fiats and a Ferrari or two are often thrown in for good measure. Talking of Fiats, the front-wheel drive saloons have a class to themselves where mildly-modified Unos are the thing to have. Support is booming with record grids in the last couple of years.

New for 2000 was the VW Cup for a wide array of VWs in various stages of development. Ventos and Golfs were the most popular, but new Beetles are expected in 2001. With the end of the Tomcat/Vento series, the VW Cup is expected to go from strength to strength in coming seasons.

A successful amalgamation of five one-make classes that formerly had manufacturer support is the Super Coupe Cup. By adding the Honda CRX, Renault 5GT Turbo and VW Polo G40, Rover 216GTi and Renault Clio classes together and tweaking the regulations to ensure parity of performance, a very cost-effective championship was created from five that would not have survived alone.

The Citroen 2CV class is among the cheapest ways of starting racing in cars that are little-modified from standard and though speeds may be slow, the class offers plenty of bumper to bumper racing. The MG Metro is not forgotten and an MG Car Club series offers a home for all sorts of Metros, from the turbo-powered racers that Rover supported in the 1980s, to road-going cars.

Finally, the Jaguar Car Club continues to encourage marque enthusiasts to race Jaguar Saloons in a championship that caters for a wide range of road-going and modified models.

7.2   SINGLE-SEATER CATEGORIES

BOSS (BIG OPEN SINGLE SEATERS)
So you want to race a Grand Prix car? This is the place for you. BOSS is, effectively, an anything goes series for single seater racing cars and includes recent era Formula 1 cars as well as Formula 3000s. Unlikely to be cheap due to the type of car involved, but if you have a burning desire to race a big, powerful single-seater, BOSS is the place.
Period racing cars will find a home with the Historic Sports Car Club in one of their classes. The Classic Racing Car series is home to all pre-'70 cars and the Derek Bell Trophy series is for all pre-'80 cars.

FORMULA 3
Still heralded as one of the best proving grounds for future Grand Prix stars, Formula 3 is Britain's premiere single seater class. It is a multi-chassis, multi-engine formula with high-tech cars powered by engines that must be production based. F3 is a highly-competitive formula with fierce competition and budgets starting from around £350,000.

For those with lesser means or ambitions, a period class called ARP Formula 3 offers amateurs the chance to race F3 cars produced prior to the end of 1997. In 2000, the class reached record grids as popularity boomed. Finally, the Historic Sports Car Club has a series for both the Toyota-powered 2-litre F3 cars of the mid-1970s and the 1600cc cars of the early 1970s.

EUROPEAN FORMULA PALMER AUDI

Formula Palmer Audi was brand new in 1998. It was the brain-child of former Grand Prix racer Jonathan Palmer who conceived a single-seater series based on the successful Barber-Dodge series in America. A field of identical Audi turbo-powered Van Diemen racing cars are prepared and delivered to the meetings by a single team. Drivers simply pay the annual fee (£125,000 for 2000) and turn up. In 2001, an increase in the number of events in Europe is planned.

FORMULA RENAULT SPORT

Renault's entry in the single-seater world underwent a fundamental change for 2000 with the introduction of a single-chassis formula. These are high-tech racing cars powered by 2-litre Renault engines and it is part of the TOCA package. In a former incarnation, Formula Renault was for 1700cc Renault-engined cars and these, along with the previous multi-marque 2-litre cars, have a lower level national championship run by the BARC.

FORMULA FORD ZETEC

The premiere Formula Ford class of the current era, with multi-chassis, slick-tyred racing cars powered by the 1800cc Ford Zetec engine. No longer a cheap way to get into racing with budgets of more than £100,000 for the top drives, but a great spring-board for the ambitious. It is part of the TOCA package, while the end of season Formula Ford Festival at Brands Hatch brings together the best of the class from all over the world.

The Junior Zetec Challenge caters for cars at least one year old. This is an excellent way into the class for those on a restricted budget and is ideal for drivers starting their single-seater careers. Year-old Zetec cars are also admitted into the Kent County Formula Ford Championship, while the BRDC Junior Single-Seater Championship is headed by Zetec-engined Formula Ford cars. New for 2000 was a club level series within the Formula 4 category from the 750MC for Zetec Formula Fords. In 2000, the Scottish championship made the switch to Zetec cars as well.

FORMULA FORD KENT

The fore-runner of Zetec and still much loved up and down the country. FF1600 (as it is known) is for spaceframe chassis single-seaters from many different manufacturers, running on a specially manufactured racing tyre and powered by the faithful Ford Kent engine. Regional or one-circuit championships are run at Brands Hatch/Lydden Hill, Oulton Park/Anglesey, Mallory Park/Silverstone/Donington and at Castle Combe. The BRDC Junior Single-Seater Championship also has a class for Kent-engined Formula Ford cars. Classes for period cars are run, namely Historic (Pre 1971), Classic (Pre 1982) and Super Classic (Pre 1990). Formula Ford continues to provide some of the best value single-seater racing available.

CLASSIC FORMULA FORD 2000
Although no longer a contemporary championship, through the 1980s Formula Ford 2000 boomed as a slicks and wings single-seater class for graduates from FF1600. Nowadays, the Classic FF2000 class caters for cars from the early 1980s and continues to provide great value for money racing for club racers. The cars are also eligible for Formula 4 (see elsewhere).

FORMULA LIBRE
Although the name is not new, the Formula Libre tag was set to be re-born in 2001 with a series of races run by the BARC and BRSCC for a range of single-seaters no longer able to sustain their own championships. The content was not confirmed at the time this publication went to press, but was expected to include cars from Formula Vauxhall, Formula Vauxhall Junior, Formula Forward, Formula EuroFirst and Europa Cup.

FORMULA HONDA
Formula 600 was created for the 1997 season with single-make racing cars powered by 600cc motorbike engines and racing on slick tyres. A step between karting and cars, the series was re-titled Formula Honda in 2000 thanks to support from the motor manufacturer. However, despite a bold re-launch and strong promotion, the series was still only attracting modest grids as the 2000 season closed.

MONOPOSTO
The Monoposto Racing Club is a bastion of single seater racing for amateurs and continues to organise a three-class championship for ex-Formula 3, Formula Renault, Formula Vauxhall, Formula Ford 2000 and Formula Ford 1600 cars. Self-built cars are also encouraged, but are increasingly rare. A new class for 1200cc motorbike-engined cars was

introduced for 2000. Cars run on slick racing tyres and are allowed wings. Monoposto is an ideal way into single-seater racing for club racers, especially those who do not necessarily want to be future Formula 1 stars!

FORMULA 4

The 750 Motor Club has owned Formula 4 for many seasons and has developed it into an excellent series for amateur racers who want to compete in single seaters with slick racing tyres and wings. Class A allows for any design of chassis, both home built and converted from F3, FF1600, FF2000 and Formula Renault. Classes B and C are for Pre '83 Formula Ford 2000 cars as raced in the Classic FF2000 series.

FORMULA VEE

This is just about as cheap as single seater racing gets! Under the protective wing of the 750 Motor Club, the class is booming with big grids and competitive racing. The class scores in having simple equipment, with the engine, gearbox and much of the suspension and braking system from the 1300 VW Beetle, mated to a spaceframe chassis. The cars run on a control Dunlop treaded tyre. A great place to start racing at very sensible cost.

7.3 SPORTS CAR CATEGORIES

GT

At the top of the sportscar tree is the BRDC GT Championship, where big-budget professional teams compete in two-driver mini-endurance races. The cars must be based on production models and classes for GT and GTO cars are included. Porsches, Chrysler Vipers and Lister Storms are among the leading cars in this high-profile championship, which is the ultimate target of many aspiring racers. Budgets start at around £50,000 per drive for a competitive car.

TVR TUSCANS

The TVR Tuscan Challenge is a crowd-pleasing series for 4500cc racing Tuscans that is always a highlight of a meeting. The teams at the front are very experienced, but in the last couple of years some of the previous front-running drivers have moved on, leaving the way open for a new generation of winners. If you have proved yourself in a lower level class, the Tuscans are a real wow to drive and it is a fine championship.

PORSCHES

The Porsche GB supported racing programme fits nicely into two categories. The Porsche Cup is for the more recent models and is a very prestigious series with some serious teams and drivers. Cars are not far removed from standard and are slotted into classes on the basis of performance rather than engine capacity. Newcomers can show well in the lesser classes, but the competition is tough. New for 2001 was the introduction of cars from the Porsche Supercup into the championship and this looks like being a highly successful move.

The Porsche Classic series provides a home for the pre '84 production racers that just seem to go on and on. Once again, the cars run in close to standard trim and the Classic series is very newcomer-friendly. A well-prepared 911 will give good value racing for year after year!

Providing entry-level racing is the Porsche 924 series which takes the plentiful, and inexpensive 924 model, and turns it into a racer with largely safety-related modifications. The action can be relatively slow compared to some classes, but good grids prove the popularity of the class which is ideal for newcomers. Also running is the Open Challenge for more modified Porsches and Ferraris.

CATERHAMS

Racing Caterhams come in many distinct varieties. Two classes are promoted by the factory while the 750 Motor Club also runs a very popular championship. Top of the pack is the Caterham Superlight R class which is no place for the faint-hearted. The 200bhp Rover K powered racer - on slicks - is a rocketship and the racing is generally frenetic.

Many people starting racing Caterhams do so in the series for Rover K powered Roadsports, which run on treaded tyres and have rather less power available. But the racing is equally close, if not closer, as great packs of cars fight it out. The Roadsport Challenge offers excellent value for money as long as your nerves can stand the level of competition and having another 25 cars in very close proximity!

The 750MC Caterham series allows K-powered cars, Ford-engined models and the near-standard cars from the former Caterham scholarship series to race together. Normally slightly less frenetic than the major national championships, this is an ideal place for novices to start learning about racing a Caterham.

The Caterham Academy run by the factory is a great way for those starting in the sport to learn, with a programme of coaching, development and speed events topped by a couple of races at the end of the season. The all-inclusive price for the scholarship is very attractive and the scheme is always sold out. Then, for those who have completed their scholarship season, the Caterham Graduate series enables them to carry on competing in subsequent seasons with the same car with a calendar largely comprised of races.

OTHER ONE-MAKE SPORTSCAR CLASSES
New onto the scene for 2000 was the Lotus Elise series which took a place on the TOCA package. The series for race prepared versions of the Rover K-powered Elise is organised on an arrive and drive basis by Lotus and the price for the season starts at around £50,000.

As you would expect, there is a class for just about every make of common sportscar. For contemporary cars, the Ginetta G27 series is for controlled examples of the 1800cc Ford-powered cars running on treaded tyres. For something rather more exotic, the Ferrari Owners' Club promotes the Ferrari Challenge which is home to both highly-modified racing specials and standard models.

MGs are immensely well-provided for on the national and club racing scene. The BARC/MG Owners' Club series is home to road-going and mildly modified versions of the Abingdon marque while the MG Car Club runs a complete cross-section of championships. The MG BCV8 series is very well established and is contested by a wide range of Bs, from the very potent and well-modified V8 racers to bog-standard Bs. There is a class for all of them, and grids are invariably full. Also now under the wing of the MG Car Club are the cars from the former high-profile MGF Cup, now running alongside less developed cars from the road-going Abingdon Trophy.

The MG Midget gets similar treatment with classes for highly-modified, mildly-modified and road-going variants in a championship that dates back more than 20 years. The road-going class, in particular, is a fine place to start racing for enthusiasts. Regional MG championships are based in East Anglia and the North West with the former admitting a wider range of cars including MG saloons.

A wide array of other marque-based sportscar classes await those keen to start racing and include series for Westfields, Morgans, Triumph TRs, Austin Healeys and Jaguars. The Jaguar Car Club also promotes the Centurian Challenge, a series of 100-mile, two-driver races for production-based sportscars. If you want to get plenty of laps for your money, this represents excellent value and also offers the chance to share your car with a fellow racer.

SPORTS RACING CARS

The Clubmans category is one of the longest established in national racing with a history of more than 30 years of racing for amateur racers who want to drive quick sports-racing cars. The front-engined heritage of the class continues in the K Sports 1600 class for spaceframe cars with slicks and wings and powered by the 1600cc Rover K engine. For high-speed cars on restricted budgets, the class has much to offer newcomers and is renowned for a friendly atmosphere. Cars from before 1980 can now join the growing Classic Clubmans movement and run with the BARC in a stand-alone series.

The National Supersports class is for rear-engined sports-racing cars, all powered by 220bhp versions of the 16-valve Vauxhall engine. Though now moving out of the range of the newcomer, the class still offers excellent speed per pound for those with a season or two of experience and who want to race a full-blown sports-racer.

Other sports-racing type classes are run by the 750 Motor Club. The roots of the 750MC are firmly based in the 750 Formula, a class for diminutive sports racing cars powered by, nowadays, 850cc Reliant engines. The driver-constructor is very much encouraged and the class has spawned some of the finest design talent the sport has seen. The class continues to be a fine home for drivers with design and engineering ability. Cars from the earlier years of the class and those based on Austin 7 components race in the 750MC Trophy series.

Big brother to F750 used to be Formula 1300 where the cars were bigger and ran 1300cc engines. However, that class has now been simply re-named Sports 2000 with the admission of former Sports 2000 cars. These are two-seat sports-racers powered by Ford engines from the class that was popular through the 1980s before fading. Now, a further Sports 2000 series has been re-created under the wing of the BRSCC, and boomed in 2000 thanks to energetic promotion by the Sports Racing Car Club.

Starting in 1999, the motorbike-engined Radical sports-racing cars had their own series under the 750MC. With cars priced at around £16,000, it represents a good way of getting into sports-racing cars for drivers of limited experience and support was excellent. For 2000, a more powerful version of the Radical was also available and a pair of series are now run for the cars. The Enduro series for the 1300cc Prosport Radicals features a number of races in Europe, most of them at around a two-hour duration.

Continuing to suffer small grids is the Global Lights class for diminutive motorbike-engined sportscars. Complete new cars are available at £15,000 but the competition from Radicals is fierce and grids remain modest. For lovers of pre-'80s sports-racing cars, the HSCC's popular RJB Thundersports series is home to the Chevrons and similar designs of the 1960s and 70s.

CLUB LEVEL GT

Not to be confused with the prestigious British GT championship, there are also GT championships for modified cars running at club level. The regulations vary across several regional or one-circuit championships but all cater for cars running with fairly extensive mods. The Castle Combe GT series has taken more of a sports-racing car route in recent years and the same regulations are used for the BRSCC's Winter GT series.

Based in the north-west, the BARC (NW) runs the Sports/Saloon challenge which keeps the more exotic machinery away and encourages modified saloons to run alongside their sportscar counterparts. The Welsh Sports/Saloon series runs to similar rules, as does the Lydden Hill series. In Scotland the Supersports/Supersaloon series continues while the re-opening of Croft has paved the way for a circuit-based series of a similar nature.

ROAD-GOING SPORTS

Despite the explosion in popularity of road-going saloon car classes, there is little mixed-marque racing for road-going sports cars. With most of the single-marque championships providing classes for road-going cars, drivers tend to shy away from mixed-marque races. However, the 750MC runs a Road Sports championship which attracts decent interest and a similar series runs at Lydden. In 2000, the Renault Spiders joined the 750MC series having been dropped from the TOCA package.

Also under the wing of the 750MC is the Kit Car series for just such cars. The more popular kits tend to dominate but some one-off machines can do well, if properly put together and driven competently. The category has boomed in recent seasons. Also under the wing of the 750MC is the Locost series for home-built sportscars produced to a set design. For 2001, a series for motorbike engined sportscars has also been introduced by the 750MC. For period cars, the Historic Sports Car Club promotes championships for Historic Road Sports and 1970s Road Sports.

OTHER HISTORIC AND CLASSIC CLASSES

Very popular with owners of fairly exotic sportscars is the Inter-Marque Challenge run by the Aston Martin Owners' Club, which pits teams of classic sportscars from Aston, Jaguar, AC, Ferrari and Porsche against each other on both a team and individual basis. The Thoroughbred Sportscar championship is run by the MG Car Club and the AMOC and is for thoroughbred and classic production road sports cars as raced in the 1950s and 1960s.

Successful recent additions to the AMOC scene are the Anglo-American Challenge and the Aston Martin Championship. The former is for pre-'70 sportscars from the USA and Britain. A wide variety of cars and full grids have typified the opening seasons. 1950s and '60s sportscars are re-created in the Sports Racing and GT Challenge series for re-works of cars raced prior to 1967. Original cars are encouraged to compete.

The HSCC also runs the Classic Sportscar series for pre-'66 sports and GT cars while the British Racing Drivers' Club promotes a high-profile series for 1950s sportscars. For anyone wishing to race older cars, the Vintage Sports Car Club is the home for any pre-war machinery, and in Scotland, the friendly Historic Ecosse series is open to any pre-'65 single-seater or sportscar.

7.4 BRITISH RACING CHAMPIONSHIPS

The following table details all current British racing championships. The columns are fairly self-explanatory, but a few notes may be useful. No individual championship sponsors are listed as they are subject to change year by year.

TYPE: this designates the type of car raced in the championship.

SLICKS: this signifies that slick racing tyres are used, but it should be noted that some championships cater for cars on both slick and treaded tyres. In these cases, a 'Yes' is recorded in the appropriate column.

WINGS: denotes that wings are permitted in the class. This is particularly relevant for single- seater classes.

SUITABLE NOVICES: In our opinion, this denotes whether the championship is suitable for novice drivers in their first season of racing. It is not a rule, merely an opinion aimed at helping novices make good decisions about where to go racing.

PRO TEAMS ONLY: This is also an opinion and denotes whether we believe the series is best suited to professional teams rather than amateurs running their own racing cars.

COST RANGE: This is a guide price range to the likely cost of buying a reasonably competitive car for the class. The key is:

A - up to £5000
B - £5000 to £10,000
C - £10,000 to £20,000
D - £20,000 to £50,000
E - Over £50,000

There will always be exceptions to this and not everyone will agree with our ratings. We have not tried to show running costs as these vary enormously from driver to driver. However, proper homework before making your selection should help you get a feel for likely costs.

ORGANISING CLUB: This is the club that organises the particular championship. Contact addresses for the various clubs can be found in Chapter 7.3

Where a decision falls between two answers, we have simply listed the answer as 'MAYBE' which is self-explanatory.

Championship	Type	Slicks	Wings	Suitable novices	Pro teams only	Cost Range	Organising Club
TOCA PACKAGE							
BTC - Touring	Saloon	Yes	Yes	No	Yes	E	TOCA
Formula Renault Sport	S/seat	Yes	Yes	No	Yes	D	BARC
BTC - Production	Saloon	Yes	No	No	No	C/D	BRDC
Renault Clio	Saloon	Yes	No	Yes	Maybe	D	BARC
Lotus Elise	Sports	Yes	No	Maybe	Yes	D	BARC
Pickup	Saloon	Yes	No	Maybe	No	C	BARC
POWERTOUR							
British GT	Sports	Yes	Yes	No	Yes	D/E	BRDC
British Formula 3	S/seat	Yes	Yes	No	Yes	D/E	BRDC
Porsche Cup	Sports	Yes	No	Maybe	No	C/D	Porsche
TVR Tuscan	Sports	Yes	No	Maybe	Maybe	C/D	BRSCC
Formula Ford Zetec	S/seat	Yes	No	Maybe	Yes	D	BRSCC
Ford Fiesta	Saloon	Yes	No	Yes	No	C	BRSCC
SINGLE SEATERS							
BOSS	S/seat	Yes	Yes	No	Maybe	D/E	BARC
ARP Formula 3	S/seat	Yes	Yes	Maybe	No	C/D	BRSCC

Championship	Type	Slicks	Wings	Suitable novices	Pro teams only	Cost Range	Organising Club
Euro Formula Palmer Audi	S/seat	Yes	Yes	No	Yes	N/a	BRSCC
BARC Formula Renault	S/seat	Yes	Yes	Yes	No	B/C	BARC
BRDC single-seater	S/seat	Yes	No	Yes	No	N/a	BRDC
Super Classic FF 1600	S/seat	No	No	Yes	No	A	BRSCC
Classic FF1600	S/seat	No	No	Yes	No	A	BARC/BRSCC
Kent County Formula Ford	S/seat	Yes/No	No	Yes	No	B	BRSCC
North West FF1600	S/seat	No	No	Yes	No	B	BRSCC
Castle Combe FF1600	S/seat	No	No	Yes	No	B	BRSCC
Star of Midlands FF1600	S/seat	No	No	Yes	No	B	BRSCC
Formula 600	S/seat	Yes	Yes	Yes	No	C	BRSCC
Classic Formula Ford 2000	S/seat	Yes	Yes	Yes	No	B/C	BARC
Monoposto	S/seat	Yes	Yes	Yes	No	B	Mono RC
Formula 4	S/seat	Yes	Yes	Yes	No	B	750MC
Formula Vee	S/seat	No	No	Yes	No	A	750MC
Junior Zetec Formula Ford	S/seat	Yes	No	Yes	No	B	BRSCC
TWMC Lydden 1600cc	S/seat	Yes	Yes	Yes	No	A	TWMC
750 MC Formula Ford Zetec	S/seat	Yes	No	Yes	No	B	750MC
Formula Libre	S/seat	Yes	Yes	Yes	No	B	BARC/BRSCC

Championship	Type	Slicks	Wings	Suitable novices	Pro teams only	Cost Range	Organising Club
SALOON CARS							
ASCAR	Saloon	Yes	No	No	Yes	D	BARC
Formula Saloon	Saloon	Yes	No	Yes	No	C/D	BARC
Mini Seven	Saloon	No	No	Yes	No	A	BRDC
Mini Miglia	Saloon	Yes	No	Yes	No	A	BRDC
Mighty Mini	Saloon	No	No	Yes	No	A	BRSCC
Super Mighty Mini	Saloon	No	No	No	No	A	BRSCC
Eurocar V8	Saloon	Yes	No	Maybe	Yes	D	BRSCC
Eurocar V6	Saloon	Yes	No	Yes	No	C	BRSCC
Legends	Saloon	No	No	Yes	No	B	BRSCC
Fiesta Si	Saloon	Yes	No	Yes	No	B	BRSCC
Modified Production/Super Road	Saloon	No	No	Yes	No	B/C	BARC
Ford Saloons	Saloon	Yes	No	Yes	No	B/C	BRSCC
VW Cup	Saloon	Yes	No	Yes	No	A/B	BRSCC
Road Saloons	Saloon	No	No	Yes	No	A	BRSCC
Super Coupe	Saloon	Yes	No	Yes	No	A	BRSCC
Castle Combe Saloon Car Cup	Saloon	No	No	Yes	No	B	BRSCC
BMW	Saloon	Yes	No	Yes	No	B/C	BARC
MG Owners Club - saloons	Saloon	No	No	Yes	No	A	BARC
Alfa Romeo	Saloon	Yes	No	Yes	No	B	BRSCC
Autoitalia	Sal/sp	Yes	No	Yes	No	B	BRSCC

Championship	Type	Slicks	Wings	Suitable novices	Pro teams only	Cost Range	Organising Club
Classic Touring Cars	Saloon	No	No	Yes	No	C/D	BARC
Group 1 Touring Cars	Saloon	No	No	Yes	No	B	BARC
Post Historic Touring Cars	Saloon	No	No	Yes	No	B	BARC
Classic & Historic Saloons	Saloon	No	No	Yes	No	B	BARC
Classic Thunder	Saloon	Yes	No	Yes	No	B/C	BARC
Ford XR (XR2 and XR3i)	Saloon	No	No	Yes	No	A	BRSCC
Hot Hatch	Saloon	No	No	Yes	No	A	750MC
Stock Hatch	Saloon	No	No	Yes	No	A	750MC
Fiats	Saloon	No	No	Yes	No	A	BRSCC
MG Metro	Saloon	Yes	No	Yes	No	A	MGCC
Citroen 2CV	Saloon	No	No	Yes	No	A	BARC
Jaguar XK Saloons	Saloon	No	No	Yes	No	B/C	Jaguar
TWMC Modified Saloons	Saloon	Yes	No	Yes	No	B	TWMC
Lydden Saloon Handicap	Saloon	Yes	No	Yes	No	A	TWMC

SPORTS CARS

Championship	Type	Slicks	Wings	Suitable novices	Pro teams only	Cost Range	Organising Club
Porsche Classic	Sports	No	No	Yes	No	B/C	Porsche
Caterham Superlight R	Sports	Yes	No	Maybe	No	C	BRSCC
Caterham 1600 Roadsport	Sports	No	No	Yes	No	B/C	BRSCC
National Supersports	Sports	Yes	Yes	Maybe	No	C/D	BRDC
K Sports 1600	Sports	Yes	Yes	Yes	No	B	BARC

Championship	Type	Slicks	Wings	Suitable novices	Pro teams only	Cost Range	Organising Club
Radicals	Sports	Yes	No	Yes	No	C	BRSCC
Ferrari	Sports	Yes	No	Yes	No	C/D	Ferrari
Ginetta	Sports	No	No	Yes	No	C	BARC
BARC (NW) Sports/Saloons	Sal/sp	Yes	No	Yes	No	B/C	BARC
Castle Combe GT	Sal/sp	Yes	No	Yes	No	B/C	BRSCC
Sports-racing & GT	Sports	Yes	No	Yes	No	B/C	BRSCC
Welsh Sports/Saloon	Sal/sp	Yes	No	Yes	No	B/C	BARC
Croft Sports/Saloons	Sal/sp	Yes	No	Yes	No	B/C	DDMC
MG Owners Club - sports	Sports	No	No	Yes	No	A	BARC
Porsche 924	Sports	No	No	Yes	No	A	BRSCC
Westfields	Sports	Yes	No	Yes	No	A/B	BARC
Morgans	Sports	Yes	No	Yes	No	B/C	Morgan
750MC Road Sports	Sports	No	No	Yes	No	B	750MC
750MC Caterham 7	Sports	Yes	No	Yes	No	B/C	750MC
750MC Kit Cars	Sports	No	No	Yes	No	A	750MC
Inter-Marque	Sports	Yes	No	Yes	No	B/C	AMOC
AMOC Anglo-American	Sports	No	No	Yes	No	B/C	AMOC
Triumph TR	Sports	No	No	Yes	No	B/C	TR Reg
Thoroughbred Sports	Sports	No	No	Yes	No	B/C	MGCC
Austin Healey	Sports	Yes	No	Yes	No	B/C	BARC
MGCC BCV8	Sports	Yes	No	Yes	No	B/C	MGCC

Championship	Type	Slicks	Wings	Suitable novices	Pro teams only	Cost Range	Organising Club
MG Midgets	Sports	Yes	No	Yes	No	A/B	MGCC
Phoenix MG	Sports	Yes	No	Yes	No	A/B	MGCC
MGCC MGF	Sports	Yes	No	Yes	No	B	MGCC
MG Cockshoot Cup	Sports	Yes	No	Yes	No	A/B	MGCC
ClubSports 2000	Sports	Yes	No	Yes	No	B	MGCC
Sports 2000	Sports	Yes	No	Yes	No	B	750MC
Formula 750	Sports	Yes	No	Yes	No	A	BRSCC
Standard/Modified Jaguars	Sports	Yes	No	Yes	No	B/C	750MC
Centurian Challenge	Sports	No	No	Yes	No	B/C	Jaguar
TWMC Lydden Sportscars	Sports	No	No	Yes	No	B	Jaguar
TWMC Lydden Special GT	Sal/sp	Yes	No	Yes	No	B	TWMC
Global Lights	Sports	Yes	No	Yes	No	C	TWMC

HISTORIC CLASSES

Championship	Type	Slicks	Wings	Suitable novices	Pro teams only	Cost Range	Organising Club
Thundersports	Sports	Yes	Yes	Yes	No	C/D	HSCC
Historic Formula 3	S/seat	Yes	Yes	Yes	No	B/C	HSCC
Classic Racing Cars	S/seat	No	No	Yes	No	B/C	HSCC
Derek Bell Trophy	S/seat	Yes	Yes	Yes	No	B/C	HSCC
Classic Clubmans	Sports	Yes	Yes	Yes	No	B/C	BARC
Historic Formula Ford 1600	S/Seat	No	No	Yes	No	B/C	HSCC

Championship	Type	Slicks	Wings	Suitable novices	Pro teams only	Cost Range	Organising Club
Classic Sports	Sports	No	No	Yes	No	B/C	HSCC
Historic Road Sports	Sports	No	No	Yes	No	B/C	HSCC
70s Road Sports	Sports	No	No	Yes	No	B/C	HSCC
Historic Racing Saloons	Saloon	No	No	Yes	No	B/C	HSCC
1950s Sportscars	Sports	No	No	Yes	No	C/D	BRDC
750MC Trophy	Sports	No	No	Yes	No	B/C	750MC
SCOTTISH CLASSES							
Scottish Formula Ford	S/Seat	Yes	No	Yes	No	B	SMRC
Scottish Road Saloons	Saloon	No	No	Yes	No	A	SMRC
Scottish XR	Saloon	No	No	Yes	No	A	SMRC
Historic Ecosse	Sp/S-s	No	No	Yes	No	B/C	SMRC
Scottish Supersaloon/sports	Sp/sal	Yes	No	Yes	No	B/C	SMRC

CHAPTER 8
APPENDICES

IN THIS CHAPTER

8.1 ARDS-RECOGNISED RACING SCHOOLS
- ➤ The complete list of schools
- ➤ Contact telephone numbers

8.2 BRITISH CIRCUITS AND TESTING FACILITIES
- ➤ The complete list of British racing circuits
- ➤ Testing information
- ➤ Contact telephone numbers
- ➤ Circuit lengths

8.3 USEFUL ADDRESSES
- ➤ Championship organisers
- ➤ Organising clubs
- ➤ Motorsport bookshops

8.4 USEFUL PUBLICATIONS
- ➤ Weekly magazines
- ➤ Monthly magazines
- ➤ Major club magazines

8.5 FLAG SIGNALS
- ➤ All current flags and their meaning

8.6 GLOSSARY
- ➤ Abbreviations used in this book

8.7 WEB SITES
- ➤ Useful web sites

8.1 ARDS-RECOGNISED RACING SCHOOLS

School name and telephone	Circuit	Principal
Aintree Racing Drivers' School 01928 712877	Three Sisters	Malcolm Barfoot
Anglesey Motor Racing School 01407 840253	Anglesey	Richard Peacock
Castle Combe Racing School 01249 782417	Castle Combe	Howard Strawford
Everyman Motor Racing 01455 841670	Mallory Park	John Farnham
Ian Taylor Motor Racing School 01264 773511	Thruxton	Bill Coombs
Jim Russell Racing Drivers' School 01509 219191	Rockingham	John Kirkpatrick
Knockhill Racing Drivers' School 01383 723337	Knockhill	Derek Butcher
Nigel Mansell Racing School 0990 125250	Brands Hatch	Tim Jones
Nigel Mansell Racing School 01829 760301	Oulton Park	Tim Jones
Nigel Mansell Racing School 01953 887303	Snetterton	Tim Jones
Richard Peacock Race School Ireland. 01232 862332	Kirkistown	Richard Peacock
Road & Track 01243 778118	Goodwood	Craig Tyler
Silverstone Drive 01327 857177	Silverstone	Paul O'Brien
Silverstone Drive at Croft 01325 722272	Croft	Paul O'Brien
Silverstone Drive at Donington 01327 857177	Donington Park	Paul O'Brien
Tom Brown Racing Drivers' School 0141 641 2553	Jurby	Tom Brown

8.2 BRITISH CIRCUITS AND TESTING FACILITIES

Race circuits in Britain

1   Knockhill
2   Kirkistown
3   Jurby
4   Croft
5   Oulton Park
6   Cadwell Park
7   Donington Park
8   Mallory Park
9   Silverstone
10 Pembrey
11 Snetterton
12 Castle Combe
13 Thruxton
14 Brands Hatch
15 Lydden
16 Anglesey
17 Goodwood
18 Three Sisters

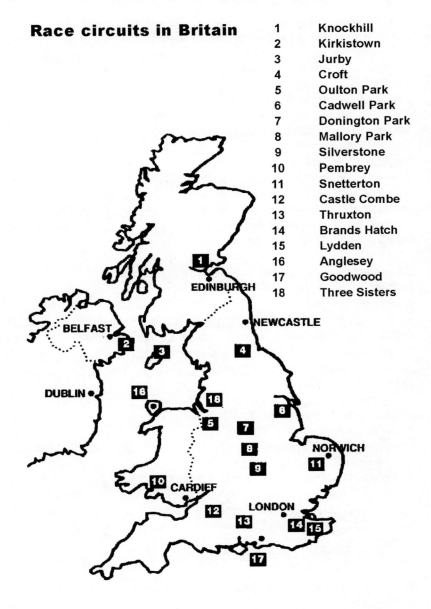

ANGLESEY, NORTH-WEST WALES. TEL 01407 840253.

1.06 miles

The circuit was inaugurated in July 1997, and is a tricky and technical circuit with spectacular backdrops. Around half a dozen race meetings each year are run at this ideal club racing venue. Though a little off the beaten track, it is a fine testing venue for those in search of very good value track time with not too many other cars. Call the above number for details of general testing.

BRANDS HATCH, KENT. TEL 01474 872331.

Grand Prix circuit - 2.6 miles

Indy circuit - 1.2 miles

One of Britain's best known circuits with a busy programme of racing and an even busier racing school. A drivers challenge on either circuit, but club racers have few chances to sample the daunting Grand Prix track. Testing is not plentiful but days are allocated for general testing. Call 01474 874817 for more information.

CADWELL PARK, LINCOLNSHIRE. TEL 01507 343248.

Full circuit - 2.17 miles

Short circuit - 1.47 miles

Britain's very own mini-Nurburgring is probably the most challenging circuit in the country. A real treat for drivers, it is popular with club racers though missed out by the major national championships. Testing is fairly regularly available and sensibly-priced. Call the above number for details of general test days.

CASTLE COMBE, WILTSHIRE. TEL 01249 782417.

1.964 miles

High-speed and bumpy, Castle Combe has a unique atmosphere with race meetings typified by bumper crowds. Changes to the circuit for 1999 saw the introduction of two ess-bands to slow speeds. Planning restrictions mean that testing is usually limited to one day per race meeting and gets booked up incredibly early - often months in advance. Call the circuit for details, but you have to plan ahead.

CROFT, NORTH YORKSHIRE. TEL 01325 721815.

2.1 miles

Re-opened and extended, Croft now brings prestige meetings to the north-east. Croft is an emerging facility with a track that offers a real challenge to racers, with a mix of just about every type of corner. It also makes a fine testing venue and reasonable prices and wide availability of testing makes it worth the trip. Ring the circuit for dates.

Donington Park, Leicestershire. Tel 01332 810048.

Grand Prix circuit - 2.5 miles
National circuit - 1.95 miles
Donington is a fine facility that is available to amateur and professional racer alike. Its central location makes it extremely popular and full grids are usually the result. Swooping down the Craner Curves into the Old Hairpin is one of the best sections of track in the UK. Testing is regularly available (usually Tuesdays and Thursdays) but very expensive! Call the circuit for dates.

Goodwood, West Sussex. Tel 01243 789660.

2.38 miles.
Until the mid-60s, when it closed on safety grounds, Goodwood was one of Britain's most popular tracks. Now, the track has been re-opened and the revival meeting in September is a huge success. However, events are likely to be restricted to one each year for historic and classic cars. Testing is available quite regularly.

Jurby, Isle of Man. Tel 01624 644644.

1.5 miles.
The Isle of Man is a wonderful place for motorsport with an enlightened approach from the local people and government. The airfield circuit at Jurby is the first step towards the creation of a permanent circuit on the island but is currently in its infancy with little in the way of facilities. Two or three meetings are planned each year and testing opportunities are based around those events.

Kirkistown, Northern Ireland. Tel 01247 771325.

1.53 miles.
Kirkistown is Northern Ireland's only race circuit and, though limited to just seven meetings a year, promotes close racing in a typically friendly atmosphere. Sadly, few mainland championships visit Kirkistown. The circuit is, however, widely available for testing most days of the week. Call the circuit office for details.

KNOCKHILL, FIFE. TEL 01383 723337.

1.3 miles.

The Scottish circuit is a demanding track that rises and falls across moorland. A lot of challenge is packed into its 1.3 miles and an annual summer visit of the BTCC is usually action-packed. Many English championships pay an annual visit to Knockhill and a warm welcome and plentiful testing makes the trip worthwhile. Good value testing is regularly available, call the circuit for details.

LYDDEN HILL, KENT. TEL 01304 830557.

1 mile.

Tucked away in a far corner of Kent, Lydden Hill has a unique character in British motor racing with a series of local championships and occasional visits from national series. For such a busy track, testing is very limited and if you miss the day or two at the start of the season, you'll be out of luck.

MALLORY PARK, LEICESTERSHIRE. TEL 01455 842931.

Full circuit - 1.35 miles
Oval - 1 mile.

A popular club racing venue, the Mallory lap is dominated by the never-ending Gerards. The Eurocar movement makes use of the one-mile oval but other meetings use the longer circuit that includes the tight Shaws Hairpin. Testing for cars is held every Wednesday morning and, though often busy, represents excellent value for money. Call the circuit to book a slot.

OULTON PARK, CHESHIRE. TEL 01829 760301.

International circuit - 2.77 miles
Fosters circuit - 1.66 miles

Oulton is not only one of the most picturesque tracks in Britain, but also one of the most demanding. The full circuit - at nearly 3 miles long - is not for the faint of heart, while the shorter Fosters track still has much to challenge drivers. Both variations are regularly used for national racing while the intermediate Island circuit is also used from time to time. Testing is vital if you are to start mastering the track and the circuit office can supply details of reasonably-priced general test days.

PEMBREY, CARMARTHENSHIRE. TEL 01554 891042.

1.45 miles

Now over ten years, old Pembrey has established itself as a national racing venue and was completely re-surfaced early in 1997. Sadly, its relatively remote location prevents some competitors from making the trip and smaller grids can be the result. That is a shame, for the circuit is a tricky one that tests man and machine with one half of the track being twisty and technical; the other half characterised by fast sweeping bends. For testing, it is one of the best with plenty of track time available at competitive rates. Call the above number for details of general test sessions.

SILVERSTONE, NORTHAMPTONSHIRE. TEL 01327 857271.

Grand Prix circuit - 3.194 miles

International circuit - 2.2 miles

National circuit - 1.64 miles

Stowe circuit - 0.79miles

Now indisputably the home of British motor racing, Silverstone is still accessible to club racers who will have occasional forays onto the International circuit and regular meetings on the national circuit. To the credit of the circuit owners, small clubs still get dates for their annual meetings on the national circuit. With a number of circuit variations available, testing is frequent. Normal general tests are Tuesday (International circuit) and Friday (National circuit), while the Stowe circuit is also used for testing and is sometimes available at short notice. Silverstone is frequently used by Formula 1 teams for testing. Check availability with the testing office on 01327 320216.

SNETTERTON, NORFOLK. TEL 01953 887303.

1.95 miles

Snetterton really is the home of testing! Its remote location and unrestricted circuit use mean that you can pound round the track virtually any day of the week. Though not as charismatic as some venues, Snetterton is an important part of British motor racing and is regularly used for national and club racing. Testing fees are competitive and if you want track time, this is one of the best places to go. Call the circuit office for testing details.

THREE SISTERS, LANCASHIRE. TEL 01942 270230.

1 mile

Though not currently home to car racing, the popular Three Sisters track is fully licensed and is often used for car testing as it is easily accessed from the M6 and testing is sensibly priced. Car testing is available on Thursday mornings and at other times subject to circuit usage. The venue is run by Malcolm Barfoot and John Hammersley, both active racers.

THRUXTON, HAMPSHIRE. TEL 01264 772696.

2.35 miles

Thruxton is a unique challenge for racers, with a series of incredibly quick sweeping corners linked by two technical sequences of corners. It is not a track easily mastered and severe planning restrictions mean that only 12 days of racing or qualifying are allowed each season. That also severely restricts testing. Club racers have to learn it on foot or through the racing school!

8.3 USEFUL ADDRESSES

Alfa Romeo Owners' Club
97 High Street
Linton
Cambs
CB1 6JT   Tel 01223 894300

Association of Racing Drivers' Schools
43 King George Gardens
Broyle Road
Chichester
West Sussex
PO19 4LB   Tel 01243 789308

Aston Martin Owners' Club
1a High Street
Sutton
Ely
Cambs
CB6 2RB   Tel 01353 777353

Big Open Single Seaters (BOSS)
Randlepike Farm
Cowers Lane
Belper
Derbyshire
DE56 2DZ   Tel 01773 550740

British Automobile Racing Club
Thruxton Circuit
Andover
Hants
SP11 8PN   Tel 01264 882200

British Motor Racing Marshals' Club
Ballaugh
27 Dollicott
Haddenham
Bucks
HP17 8JL   Tel 01844 290631

British Motor Sports Association for the Disabled
PO Box 120
Aldershot
Hants
GU11 3TF   Tel 01252 319070

British Racing Drivers' Club
Silverstone Circuit
Towcester
Northants
NN12 8TN   Tel 01327 857271

British Racing & Sports Car Club
35 Kings Hill Avenue
West Malling
Kent
ME19 4RR   Tel 01732 848884

Chaters Motoring Booksellers
8 South Street
Isleworth
Middlesex
TW7 7BJ   Tel 020 8568 9750

Darlington & District Motor Club
15 Oakdene Avenue
Darlington
Co. Durham
DL3 7HR   Tel 01325 484829

Demon Tweeks
75 Ash Road South
Wrexham Ind Estate
Wrexham
North Wales
LL13 9UG   Tel 01978 664466

Ferrari Owners' Club
Chevy Chase
145b Leeds Road
Selby
Yorks
YO8 0JH   Tel 01757 290547

500 Motor Racing Club of Ireland
Kirkistown Race Circuit
Rubane Road
Kircubbin
Newtonards
Co Down
BT22 1AU   Tel 01247 771325

Historic Sports Car Club
Silverstone Circuit
Towcester
Northants
NN12 8TN   Tel 01327 858400

MG Car Club
Kimber House
PO Box 251
Abingdon
Oxon
OX14 1FF   Tel 01235 555552

Mill House Books
The Mill House
Eastville
Boston
Lincs
PE22 8LS   Tel 01205 270377

Monoposto Racing Club
The Nook
Rodborough Common
Stroud
Glos
GL5 5BU   Tel 01453 873654

Morgan Sports Car Club
Lintridge Farm
Bromsberrow Heath
Ledbury
Herefordshire
HR8 1PB   Tel 01531 650760

Motor Sports Association
Motorsports House
Riverside Park
Colnbrook
Slough
SL3 0HG   Tel 01753 681736

Porsche Club GB
Hay Barn
Manor Farm
East Lavant
Chichester
West Sussex
PO18 0AH   Tel 01243 538911

Scottish Motor Racing Club
2 Mayfield Mews
Falkirk
FK1 5SP   Tel 01324 625456

750 Motor Club
West View
New Street
Stradbrooke
Eye
Suffolk
IP21 5JG   Tel 01379 384268

TR Register
Hollybush Cottage
Norbury
Whitchurch
Shropshire
SY13 4PW   Tel 01948 663827

Tunbridge Wells Motor Club/
South-East Motorsport Enthusiasts Club (SEMSEC)
46 Rochester Way
Crowborough
East Sussex
TN6 2DT   Tel 01892 655978

8.4 USEFUL PUBLICATIONS

Autosport
The weekly magazine for the sport, covering national and international sport.
Published every Thursday.
Haymarket Publishing, 38-42 Hampton Road, Teddington, Middx, TW11 0JE.
Tel 020 8943 5000.

Autosport Guide
The complete guide to driving on all UK (and some European) circuits, with a corner by corner narrative and accompanying diagrams.
What's On Motor Sport Ltd, Newbarn Court, Ditchley Park, Chipping Norton, Oxon, OX7 4EX.
Tel 01993 891000.

British Racing News
The monthly magazine of the British Racing and Sports Car Club.
TFM Publishing, Brimstree View, Kemberton, Shifnal, Shropshire, TF11 9LL.
Tel 01952 583104.

Cars and Car Conversions
A monthly magazine covering fast road cars and competition cars. Includes lots of technical features and good information about getting started in motorsport.
IPC Media, Dingwall Avenue, Croydon, Surrey, CR9 2TA.
Tel 020 8686 2599.

Motoring News
The weekly newspaper for the sport, covering national and international sport.
Published every Wednesday.
Motoring News, Somerset House, Somerset Road, Teddington, Middx, TW11 8RU.
Tel 020 8267 5385

Motor Sport
A monthly magazine, covering national and international sport with a particular emphasis on retro features.
Haymarket Publishing, 38-42 Hampton Road, Teddington, Middx, TW11 0JE.
Tel 020 8943 5000.

Motorsports Now
The official publication of the governing body of British motorsport.
Motor Sports Association, Motorsports House, Riverside Park, Colnbrook, Slough, SL3 0HG.
Tel 01753 681736.

Racecar Engineering

A monthly magazine devoted to the engineering and technical side of motorsport.
IPC Media, Dingwall Avenue, Croydon, Surrey, CR9 2TA.
Tel 020 8686 2599.

Racetech Magazine

A monthly magazine devoted to the engineering and technical side of motorsport.
4 Church Close, Whetstone, London, N20 0JU.
Tel 020 8368 4121.

Startline

The monthly magazine of the British Automobile Racing Club.
BARC, Thruxton Circuit, Andover, Hants, SP11 8PN.
Tel 01264 882200.

8.5 FLAG SIGNALS

The definitive description of flag signals will be found in the MSA 'Blue Book'. This should be consulted at all times.

The following flag signals may be displayed at the start/finish line:

Red flag: the race or qualifying session has been stopped. No overtaking.
Green flag: the start of a formation lap.
Black flag with orange disc and white number: there is a mechanical problem or fire on your car that you may not be aware of. Driver must call at his pit on the next lap.
Black and white diagonally split flag and white number: your driving is suspect and you are being observed.
Black flag with white number: driver must stop at the pits within one lap.
Black and white chequered flag: end of race or qualifying session.
Black and yellow quartered flag: race neutralised, slow down and form up behind race leader. No overtaking.

The following flag signals may be displayed at marshals' posts around the circuit:

Red flag: the race or qualifying session has been stopped. No overtaking.
Blue flag (stationary): another competitor is following you closely.
Blue flag (waved): another competitor is trying to overtake you.
White flag: a slow moving car or service vehicle is on the track.
Yellow flag (stationary): danger, slow down, no overtaking.
Yellow flag (waved): great danger, slow down considerably, be prepared to stop, no overtaking.
Yellow flag with red stripes: slippery surface.
Green flag: all clear at the end of a danger area controlled by yellow flags. The green flag is also shown for the first lap of qualifying and during the formation lap of the race.
Hazard board: a warning of a hazard that was not present when the practice session or race commenced.
Black and yellow quartered flag: race neutralised, slow down and form up behind race leader. No overtaking.

Additionally, a hazard board may de displayed at marshals' posts comprising a black triangle containing an exclamation mark on a yellow background. This denotes a hazard that was not present when the qualifying session or race started.

8.6 GLOSSARY

AMOC	Aston Martin Owners' Club
ARDS	Association of Racing Drivers' Schools
BARC	British Automobile Racing Club
BOSS	Big Open Single Seaters
BRDC	British Racing Drivers' Club
BRSCC	British Racing and Sports Car Club
BTCC	British Touring Car Championship
CoC	Clerk of the Course
DDMC	Darlington & District Motor Club
FIA	Federation Internationale de l'Automobile

HSCC	Historic Sports Car Club
MGCC	MG Car Club
MSA	Motor Sports Association
NDTC	Novice Driver Training Course
SMRC	Scottish Motor Racing Club
TOCA	Touring Car Association
TWMC	Tunbridge Wells Motor Club
500MRC	500 Motor Racing Club of Ireland

8.7 WEB SITES

CLUBS AND ASSOCIATIONS

750MC **www.750mc.co.uk**
BARC **www.barc.net**
BRDC **www.silverstone-circuit.co.uk/brdc**
BRSCC **www.brscc.co.uk**
British Women Racing Drivers' Club **www.bwrdc.co.uk**
Classic Saloon Car Club **www.csccgb.co.uk**
FIA **www.fia.com**
Formula 3 Association **www.fota.co.uk**
Motor Sports Association **www.msauk.org**

RACING SCHOOLS

Aintree Racing Drivers' School **www.aintree-racing-drivers-school.co.uk**
Nigel Mansell Racing School **www.brands-hatch.co.uk**
Castle Combe Racing School **www.combe-events.co.uk**
Jim Russell Racing Drivers' School **www.jimrussell.co.uk**
Knockhill Racing School **www.knockhill.co.uk**
Silverstone Drive **www.silverstone-circuit.co.uk**
Ian Taylor Motor Racing School **www.iantaylor.co.uk**

RACE CIRCUITS

Brands Hatch **www.brands-hatch.co.uk**
Cadwell Park **www.brands-hatch.co.uk**
Castle Combe **www.castlecombecircuit.co.uk**
Croft **www.croftcircuit.co.uk**
Donington Park **www.donington-park.co.uk**

Goodwood **www.goodwood.co.uk**
Knockhill **www.knockhill.co.uk**
Lydden Hill **www.eyecue.co.uk/semsec**
Mallory Park **www.mallorypark.co.uk**
Oulton Park **www.brands-hatch.co.uk**
Pembrey **www.barc.net**
Silverstone **www.silverstone-circuit.co.uk**
Snetterton **www.brands-hatch.co.uk**
Three Sisters **www.aintree-racing-drivers-school.co.uk**
Thruxton **www.barc.net**

RACE CHAMPIONSHIPS
2CV **www.2cvracing.co.uk**
Caterham Challenges **www.caterham.co.uk**
Caterham Graduates **www.graduates.org.uk**
Classic FF2000 **www.ursff2000.freeserve.co.uk**
Eurocar **www.eurocar-racing.com**
Europa Cup **www.euro-racing.com**
Formula Palmer Audi **www.jpalmer.com**
Formula Saloons **www.formulasaloons.com**
K Sports 1600 **www.ksports1600.org.uk**
Legends **www.legends-cars.com**
Maranello Ferrari Challenge **www.ferrariownersclub.co.uk**
MG Owners Club **www.mgcars.org.uk**
Mighty Minis **www.mighty-minis-racing.co.uk**
Mini Seven and Miglia **www.mini7.co.uk**
Monoposto Racing Club **www.monoposto.freeserve.co.uk**
Morgan Challenge **www.mkurrein.co.uk/mmcc**
Porsche Cup and Classic **www.msdpcgb.co.uk**
Radicals **www.radicalms.co.uk**
Scottish FF Zetec **www.scottish-zetec.co.uk**
Sports 2000 **www.sports2000-srcc.com**
TVR Tuscans **www.tvr-tuscan.co.uk**
VW Cup **www.vw-cup.co.uk**

GENERAL INFORMATION
Autosport **www.autosport.com**
British Motor Racing Circuits **www.bmrc.co.uk**

Go Motorsport **www.go-motorsport.co.uk**
Motorsport On Line **www.motorsportonline.co.uk**
PowerTour **www.powertour.co.uk**
Race Car New Media **www.racecar.co.uk**
Sportscar World **www.supersportscarworld.com**
Ten Tenths **www.ten-tenths.com**
The Grid **www.thegrid.co.uk**
UK Motorsport **www.ukmotorsport.com**